TRIAL BY TRIAL

TRIAL BY TRIAL

DON STEPHENS

HARVEST HOUSE PUBLISHERS
Eugene, Oregon 97402

TRIAL BY TRIAL

ACKNOWLEDGEMENTS

The writing of this manuscript has made me aware of the many who helped me in my life. It is customary for an author to thank those who helped him with his book but I want to also recognize and express my gratitude for my true friends—those who believed in me when the going was tough. Thank you to the members of the International Council of Youth With A Mission: Loren Cunningham, Leland Paris, Floyd McClung, Jim Dawson, Jim Rogers, Kalafi Moala, and Wally Wenge.

I want to thank the gang from the early days in Europe, those who believed with me for the ship: Lynn Green, Dave Boyd, Wilbert Van Laake, Jeff Fountain, Tom Bloomer, Iain Muir, Al Akimoff, Mark Spengler, Albert Joly, Heinz Suter, Daniel Schaerer, Joe Portale, Doug Sparks, Rudi Lack, Charles Vichoud, Tom Bragg, Tom Jennings, Volker Embgen, Keith Warrington, Barry Austin, Oliver Nyumbu, Larry Wright, Jan Helge Froen, Christian Westergaard, Teemu Ylipahkala, and Steve Goode.

I am grateful to my old friends in Lausanne, Switzerland who gradually released me as their director and let me go to the ship. They were patient and loyal. Their sacrifice has blessed many.

To the thousands of YWAM staff worldwide, who gave, prayed, and believed with us for the resurrection of a dream, I cannot find words that say how much their participation sustained and strengthened me.

It has been my privilege in 17 years in the organization, 21 years since my first summer of service, to have been blessed with talented and capable secretaries and assistants: Charlene Jennings, Marie Goode, Janet Potter, Heather Choate, and especially Landa Cope, Patty Wilkenson, and Simonne McCluskey.

On the ships, we have some of the most dedicated people in the world. In the long haul from a dream to reality, they stood with me. Many of them are truly among God's best. Captain Ben and Helen Applegate, Alan and Fay Williams, Jack and Myrna Hill, Dave and Linda Cowie, Rene and Marianne Lako, Denis and Heather Choate, John and Marion Brignall, David and Gigi O'kane, Jim and Judy Orred, Nick and Rozanne Savoca, and Rich and Cheryl Mackey have all been important parts of the leadership team. As in any story, it is not one individual but the team who loyally support their leader that really get things done. All of these are doers and not talkers. There are another 200 who should be listed here as they are the real backbone of the mercy ships. Thank you to each one who stands beside me.

Joy Dawson and Jean Darnall are two ladies who must be mentioned, along with Darlene Cunningham and my mother: By their example they influenced me to know God.

My publisher, Bob Hawkins at Harvest House, and his staff, certainly Eileen Mason and Lela Gilbert have all done the impossible. Their reputation for quality publishing is well deserved.

And, I gladly thank my new friend Ed Steele, a master in the communication business, for his gentle but decisive organization of everything.

My parents, Paul and Jean Stephens, and my wife's parents, Charles and Janice Green, have been outstanding life models of integrity and dedication. My brother, Gary, and his wife, Helen, along with my sister, Joan Stephens Hadly, and her husband, David, are all a part of me and my life. Gary and Joan are each part of the tapestry of my earliest lessons. We learned them together.

But, most of all, I thank my wife, Deyon, and the children, Heidi, Luke, John Paul, and Charles who are really my whole life. Their love for me and belief in me encourage me to keep following Him in this modern Greek odyssey. They share with me the belief that God is totally trustworthy and our future is best when left completely in His hands.

CHAPTER
ONE

GUILTY!

The word sent explosive tremors through the packed Athens courtroom. Instead of fear and intimidation, new courage gripped the trio on trial as well as the curious, supportive onlookers. Spontaneously, slowly at first, they all began to applaud! Somehow an American and a New Zealander standing beside their Greek friend had transformed the small, flickering spark of hope for freedom into a mighty burst of flame. And although the court's decision was transparently unjust, the Greek believers who crowded the little room knew it would bring their own personal persecutions before the eyes of the world.

Soon that newly kindled tongue of fire would surprise everyone. It would not be stamped out. It would refuse to die. The winds of adversity would blow, yet the howling opposition would only fan the blaze into shining brilliance.

The presiding judge wrinkled his brow in perplexity. What was he thinking? "I sentence you to 4½ years in prison for proselytizing."

Now pandemonium broke out in the crowded court. No matter that it was only two days before Christmas Eve and its usual celebrations.

The fifth district Athens court had seemed cold and foreboding in the early morning hours. Yet at this moment, after 15 hours of grueling questions and the various posturings of the four attorneys, raw emotion prevailed. Our translator simply stopped speaking. The sound was deafening. Everyone seemed to be speaking all at once.

At last the presiding judge called for order again. A quiet hush fell over the place. The Acropolis with its tradition of historic freedoms and ideals seemed light-years away. For here, in the very shadow of the birthplace of democracy, three men were being condemned for charges that stemmed from giving a 16-year-old boy a book. The judge peered over the top of that book. In an unexpected display of leniency, he reduced the sentence to 3½ years.

I glanced at Alan and Costas. How were they feeling? What thoughts were racing through the passages of their minds? What would I tell my precious wife, Deyon, exactly halfway around the world in Hawaii?

I pictured the faces of each of my four children. How would their father being in a Greek jail affect them? What about the 200 loyal crew members on the mercy ships? How would they feel? Would my children ever respect me as a father? Would the ships ever sail again?

Then I thought of my father.

Dad had always stressed character and a good name. Diligence and hard work were in his blood. His grandfather had been of pioneer stock. Hardships in taming a wild part of the Rocky Mountains had put staying power in their very bones.

Now, as the judge's words faded in my ears, many of Dad's words echoed in my memory: "When you start something, make sure you finish it." How would I ever finish this? What would it mean to finish? Deep down within me there welled up a wave of emotion for my father. Would I embarrass him?

He knew the shame of having his parents fight and finally divorce. Their private relationship, that of man and wife, had broken into an open quarrel. Their caustic public remarks had somehow withered the heart of the boy, my father. He had been deeply humiliated.

Now would I be doing the same thing to my father? Would this Greek episode shame him once again?

A few days later I would telephone him. After briefly explaining the situation, I would finally gather the courage to ask the question. "Dad, have I embarrassed you? I know you didn't ever expect one of your children to be in prison."

The phone went silent. I held my breath for several seconds. Then Dad spoke: "No, Son, you haven't embarrassed me or the family. It is an honor to have you as my son. Thank you for standing for principle."

How removed that dreary courtroom was from my colorful childhood in western Colorado! There

I had grown up in the ranching and farming tradition of the Uncompahgre Plateau, a remote, rugged part of the world.

As a 9-year-old, my birthday surprise was a two-year-old unbroken sorrel stallion colt. Dad worked with me to teach both the colt and his son the meaning of responsibility. In the words of the "Old West," a colt had to be "broken" to ride. The animal and I both learned what it meant to be trained.

Any animal has a tendency to reject the will of a master. To win the confidence of the colt and to develop him to his full potential was the challenge. This would have been far too much for a young boy on his own. Only with my father there, instructing and encouraging, was it possible.

Later I often marveled at Dad's wisdom. The boy was being trained, not the colt. Had my father seen so clearly into the future some of the challenges God would place on my heart for the world He so loved? Probably not. Yet the Lord, in His wisdom and knowledge, was planning even then.

One of my greatest boyhood joys arrived when Dad and his brother moved the cattle from their winter valley pasture to summer grazing lands in the high country.

This meant a whole week off from school, riding my own horse. Camping out under the vast open skies with no pollution or noise, the silence was so intense that it was often difficult to sleep during the first nights. I awoke to the smell of a wood fire and early-morning coffee kept bubbling hot for the men. Breakfast in the woods with the background bawling of cattle made boxes of cereal eaten in suburban kitchens seem so plastic and shallow.

My uncle's place was just past the "four mile corner" and the old stone schoolhouse. There the cattle were gathered and started up the Transfer Road toward the Seliska Ranger Station, Iron Springs, and their summer pasture. All of us cousins, brothers, and nephews enjoyed every second of this. We would savor the flavor of those days for the rest of our lives.

The Continental Divide stretches along the spine of the Rocky Mountains from Canada to Mexico. It separates the great watersheds. In that region the smallest of raindrops, falling only a few inches away from each other, end up in different oceans on opposite sides of the continent. Some of these droplets form mountain streams flowing east toward the Gulf of Mexico and the Atlantic. Others find their way into the Pacific.

Little did I realize that I too would follow those same mountain streams and find myself at home in several of the world's port cities. I have known since understanding came alive in my own personality, that God had a special purpose for my life. He really plans destiny for all who will follow. I thought of all I had learned from my father.

"Speak your mind, Son. Let me know what is inside—then we can deal with it." Dad had no trouble in being candid. And he expected the same honest, open communication from his children.

"The best things in life are worth working for. Struggle. Keep on going. Don't quit. Never give up." The characteristic of perseverance is as common as blue jeans to Western folk. Unfortunately, it seems to be on the endangered species list for many others. Western people live with adversity as a way of life.

The cold winters, the unpredictability of weather, with early frosts that can ruin an orchard harvest in a few minutes—all of these place a bulldog ability in most people to never quit.

Westerners are realists but rarely cynical. Nature is too awesome and all-powerful in its revelation to produce cynics. Most have a tender heart under a leathery exterior. That was my father.

Meanwhile, Mother was his complement. Her father had come over on a steamer from Norway as a 9-year-old. Grandfather was a God-fearing Lutheran who lived by the Book. He was broad-minded before the words "interdenominational" or "ecumenical" ever became popular. He loved people and he lived an exemplary life of integrity bathed in compassion.

Grandfather thought nothing of riding horseback to neighboring farms and ranches to read and pray with other God-fearing men. It didn't matter which "brand" they rode for—Baptist, Pentecostal, or Lutheran. It *did* matter greatly that they were God-fearing, loved the Book, and respected God's people.

An ill-advised abortion in the 1930's robbed him of his lovely wife and left him with four daughters and a son. To make matters worse, in her senior year of high school his third daughter died of typhoid fever. Mother's older sister raised the family.

These people were never bitter. As a child I marveled at the healing that comes when people turn to God in their grief and sorrow. The family was so wholesome, so loving, always wanting to believe the best about everyone. Mother was the model of this. She had her father's love for prayer and the Book. She was a perfect counterpart to Dad's flinty, discerning character. Mother's prayers shaped the destiny of her sons and daughter. They strengthened us, guided us, corrected us, and helped to redeem us.

In my eighteenth year, when all the world's youths seem to need to confirm their manhood, I was in a local bar with some of my friends. Novices trying to act like addicts, we had bought the style that Madison Avenue portrayed as very macho.

Actually most of us as 17- and 18-year-olds could have shown Madison Avenue much about masculinity and maturity. But instead, the power of the media had slowly eroded our foundation of independence. By now we wanted to be conformists.

After we had been in the bar for an hour or so, one of my friends came and called me to the window. The picture I saw there is forever engraved upon my memory. It so totally disarmed my adolescent pride that I would always remember that night in shame, not glory.

Across the road was our car, parked conspicuously on the main street of the little Western town. At the wheel sat my mother. Everyone would be walking by that Saturday evening. Most would know her well. She didn't care. A battle was waging for the destiny of her son. She had brought him into this world and would not now easily lose him to the temptations of alcohol and a loose lifestyle.

So in her car on Main Street, in front of any who cared to watch, mother kept her vigil with bowed head, praying for her firstborn. She knew that eternity was holding court.

One attorney was presenting his case for abandoning the principles of integrity, wholesomeness, and belief in God. The other was reminding of all that the Book and church and family had held high for centuries.

In an instant I was totally alert. Nothing was dulled through excess of alcohol. My mother loved me enough to suffer embarrassment and to pray in a public place for my destiny! I quickly exited through a back door and drove home.

Mother never mentioned the incident for 20 years, yet she knew in her heart she had won.

For every young person, life requires the crossing of many a hazardous canyon. The path makes its way over a swinging bridge, suspended high above treacherous cataracts and white water rushing far below. The two banisters or side ropes are of paramount importance. If the swinging bridge has only one handrope, the chances of crossing are diminished by half.

The first banister is *discipline.* If a child is not corrected with loving guidelines, he never learns right from wrong, and he has no clearly defined limits. Good and evil become confused. Loving correction and discipline are absolutely required to give boundaries and balance.

Encouragement is the second banister. Someone must tell us he believes in us. My father never let his children use the words ''I can't.'' ''Can't never did anything,'' was his favorite Western proverb.

"You'll never know unless you try. It is better to try and fail than to fail to try."

My high school basketball coach provided an added boost in the area of confidence.

Our team was the worst in the league. We lost more games than any other team. None of us was even six feet tall—we were small and intimidated. Coach began to take us back to the basics. Drill. Practice. Strive for excellence. Do it right the first time. Do it so many times that it becomes automatic.

If we won our weekend game, then Monday practice was even tougher. "Don't get overconfident! Drill! Practice! Do it better. Teamwork. Pass the ball. You are five together, not alone. Work together. Help each other!" And we began to win.

Coach wasn't just training ballplayers; he was training men. If we broke training we were out. He knew the two banisters well: *Discipline* and *Encouragement.*

It was the granite bedrock foundation poured into my life by many others that gave me strength that day in the Athens court. I knew my mother was praying, just as she had prayed when I was 18. Many others had joined in prayer also. *God give me courage, help me stand. May all my answers be 100 percent true.* I wasn't the only one on trial there. The three judges, the lawyers, the plaintiff—all of us were being watched by the one true Judge. What will He ultimately say about each of our performances?

CHAPTER TWO

Even before my testimony began, people had repeatedly asked me the same question: What had brought the three of us to this Athenian trial in the first place?

I had been to Greece six or seven times over the course of ten years. Our family had driven from Cap Sounion, Corinth, and part of the Peloponnesus. We had traveled through Katarini, Thessaloniki, and Kavalla, along the same Appian Way that the apostle Paul had once traversed. We had eventually made our way into Istanbul, the ancient Constantinople.

While waiting in the dismal courtroom, I pictured countless picturesque Greek villages with whitewashed houses surrounded by bustling markets that spilled into the village squares. These provided a stark contrast to the lapis lazuli waters of the Aegean Sea.

Villages such as these have produced some of the world's great shipping magnates. Names like

Niarchos, Onassis, and Chandris are recognized in homes around the globe. Shipping, world trade, nautical know-how—these are the pride of the Greek people. And fittingly, a ship had brought me to Greece—a missionary ship.

But the story of that ship begins more than 20 years earlier in western Colorado. During those youthful days I knew that one day God would have something special for me to do. That concept had been clearly in my mind since childhood. I was simply waiting for the right person to come along, to offer me my particular opportunity for service.

At about this time I met Loren Cunningham, the founder of a work affectionately called YWAM: Youth With A Mission. Loren was ten years and 17 days my senior. We would become almost like brothers.

I was electrified the first time I heard him speak. Through the word pictures he painted, the world became alive with potential, action, excitement, and sacrifice. I was aware of nothing but the message and the kind eyes of the messenger. Their twinkle spoke of humor, fun, and an intriguing future.

Suddenly I was aware that I was being challenged by God, not Loren. It was divine providence bringing me face-to-face with the very purpose of my birth. The prayers of my grandparents, parents, and others seemed to be reaching deeply into my heart, calling me to an eternal purpose.

Here was the challenge I had been waiting for!

No self-respecting Western youth can ever walk away from a challenge. He would be branded for the rest of his life. And this challenge was far different from any youthful exploit. The cost was far greater, the consequences far more important. If I accepted this call it would radically alter my future.

At that moment it seemed as if I stood at the very top of the highest Colorado mountain. Gravity was pulling me in opposite directions. If I went for this challenge, then I, too, would join one of those small streams that make up part of a mighty river that eventually will cover the whole earth.

I knew that the challenge was not really just for the few weeks that Loren was requesting; it would be for a lifetime. I knew that to answer this challenge probably meant setting my sails for new horizons. Facing the unknown was exciting, but personal price was also staring me full in the face.

Count the cost. I tried to. And I found myself asking God for an indication beyond my own subjective reasoning.

Loren's sparkling wife, Darlene, came timidly up to me at the close of the service. "I've never done anything like this before," she smiled, "but God told me clearly to speak to a young man in a green cardigan . . . and you're the only one here in green! I'm not even sure what He wants me to say. . . ."

"You've said enough!" I was awestruck.

She couldn't have known that as I bowed in prayer I had asked God to send either Loren or Darlene to confirm my decision. Aside from a friend who sat beside me, I was a total stranger in that meeting. Only God Himself could have directed Darlene Cunningham my way.

A few nights later and 250 miles away, a vivacious

blonde named Deyon Green also agreed to spend a few weeks in God's service.

I had met Deyon nine months earlier. Several of my friends were at a youth gathering. Skip Weisbrod from the uranium mining town of Nucla was sitting next to a cute young lady. Arriving late, I slipped into the seat next to him.

The choir was already singing. My eyes surveyed the four rows of faces and focused abruptly on the blonde in the second row. Her smile and sincerity were obvious. Something about her whole person strongly attracted me to her. She seemed so very alive.

Skip leaned over and asked why I was the only one without a young lady sitting beside me? I motioned to the one in the choir. "What's her name?"

"She's spoken for," Skip chuckled.

"All the better," I grinned back. Most people have an eye for quality—it is rarely unspoken for.

In a few minutes the choir was finished. One by one the singers made their way back into the meeting. I stepped into the aisle in front of Deyon and asked if she would like to sit with me. She agreed. That's how I met my wife.

She and I were destined for the same young and unknown organization, YWAM. We would embark upon a two-month adventure in the Caribbean Islands. That was what Loren had asked us all to do—give a summer to God.

For the mission this was the "first wave." We would join 120 others for the three-month stint. In years to come, 15 to 20 thousand college-age young men and women would join in the movement. Missiologists would record a new phenomenon in the development of missions. Their conclusion was staggering—80 percent of all career missionaries got their start after short-term exposure to mission experiences!

The development of the concept made sense. It was terribly expensive to prepare and train an adult family, then to support them on location for four or five years. More costly was the fact that a significant percentage of these did not return for a career. The idea of using unmarried, college-age candidates was a good one.

Twenty years ago such innovation was unheard of and even controversial. Nevertheless, I sensed that seeds of greatness lay within many of the dedicated souls I worked with shoulder-to-shoulder in the Caribbean. Our goal was to reach every home on every island with a Bible or a piece of gospel literature.

Several things happened during that summer of 1964. I knew that God had called me to help the helpless. I didn't want to do it alone. Deyon and I spent only a brief time together that summer, but our hearts were knit. We would follow God's call—and we would follow it together.

I had watched my parents carefully. In 19 years I could remember only one disagreement between them; our home had harmony. Mother always said, "It is easier to *keep* peace than to *make* peace." She was a peacekeeper. She also had her father's compassionate heart.

Often we would prepare "care packages" for less fortunate families. We would deliver them on Sunday morning. At that time we asked if any of the children would like to go to church with us. Mother taught us to care, and to put our care into action.

She was faithful to lead us in prayer every night. Rarely did we miss gathering around the Book. My earliest memories still echo the Bible stories that Mother read to us.

This was the kind of family life I wanted to share with Deyon. For that spiritual nurturing had led me to the islands of the Caribbean.

Our team was at Mangrove Cay on Andros Island. House to house we tramped with our Christian literature. Every footstep seemed to lead me further from the mountains of my childhood into the seas of adventure. Our team was led by an islander named Moxie. Somehow, through our novitiate efforts, God allowed us to birth a new church through the converts of the island.

It amazed me to see the power of God working through young lives like my own. We were on a steep learning curve. The knowledge gained there would be a helmsman through future storms and turbulent waters.

Like a symbol of those impending difficulties, Hurricane Cleo swooped down on our defenseless islands at the summer's end. Water ran high in the streets. Palm trees crashed into the landscape. Power lines were down, some writhing snakelike in their electricity before fuses gave way at a distant control panel.

People were devastated. Homes were destroyed. What could we do? All our efforts of the summer seemed so thimblelike compared with the human need that surrounded us now. There, in a prayer meeting, a girl prayed a simple prayer. She asked God to someday give His people a ship—a ship with doctors, nurses, medicines, food, and materials. In this way He could bring His heart to troubled, hurting people.

As she spoke, I thought of the example of my mother and the care boxes. It was the same principle: People know that God loves them through the actions of His followers.

What we have to say is often not enough; our words must be accompanied by our efforts. *"Use two hands,"* mother would say. One hand holds the gospel—the good news. The other hand meets the practical needs of food for the hungry, clothing for the devastated, medicine and healing for the hurting. Two hands, practical and powerful. Hearts and hands together in Jesus' name. Balance. Not just one hand giving social help, but two hands also giving spiritual help. Social and spiritual. Practical and personal. Temporal and eternal. Words and deeds. Hearts and hands.

There are nearly 3 million people in this world who have never heard the gospel—not even once. Meanwhile in some cities tens of thousands of street orphans scavenge for food and shelter. In Calcutta alone over a million people come into the world, then live and die, with the same filthy street as their only home. Both hands are needed. And the workers are few.

Eighteen years after my "initiation" in the Caribbean, I met Keith and Melody Green at their center in Texas. There was an immediate bonding. The fire of God burned in this powerful musician's heart. He wanted to be exposed to the needs of the world and to missions. Quickly I arranged for Keith and Melody to visit four of the mission centers and then the ship.

We strategized, discussed, prayed, and had fun together. In a prayer meeting under the open sky of the Mediterranean, we prayed for the world. Keith began to be burdened in a new way. Here is what he later wrote in an article (one of his last):

> As I travelled from country to country, I thought of the millions of people I was passing through who needed to have the Gospel of Jesus shown to them in a real way—and yet, there was hardly anyone there to reach them.
>
> There are over two billion, seven hundred thousand people who have never heard the Gospel at all. There are only five to seven thousand missionaries worldwide working directly with these totally unreached groups of people. This means there is approximately *one missionary for every four hundred and fifty thousand people.* . . . While we in America have approximately *one worker for every two hundred and thirty people.*
>
> Last Days tract by Keith Green

Keith's heart had been stirred by God. The conclusion is obvious to even the untrained eye: Tens of thousands of young people need to give God a summer in exposure to missions.

Exposure missions can be called the "boot camp" of candidate training—it is usually a make it or break it situation. Some excel under the discipline and demands, and others can't wait until it is over. A seed is planted and, in the winds of adversity, roots go down deep for God.

The candidate experiences firsthand the obstacles, cultural differences, and challenges. The rigidity of age has not yet so set his mindframe as to prohibit total identity with different cultural settings.

Exposure missions can be as dry as the Sahara desert, as demanding as the ascent of Everest, and as difficult as escaping from Alcatraz. Some short-term teams have all of these, while others seemingly have it easy. They return rejoicing. God determines the mix: He is in control and through each experience, we have something to learn.

This was what our summer in the Caribbean was all about. Along with our colleagues, Deyon and I were exposed to man's deepest physical and spiritual needs. We would never be the same again.

What did we learn? The lessons were many. But certain principles have remained with us ever since.

First Efforts

God is interested in proving what His new recruits are made of. Are there any Daniels who will refuse tempting palace food, later to shut the mouths of lions? Are there any Josephs who will allow prison to become an avenue for the release of God's promises? Are there any Absaloms who will betray even their own family for the sake of power?

First efforts are risky. Each candidate faces firsthand the obstacles, cultural differences, and trials that always accompany mission work. Everything he will encounter in years to come presents itself in miniature during those early days.

Teamwork

God uses teams. One of the greatest testimonies of teamwork is the Billy Graham Evangelistic Association. These men have worked side by side for years. It is not one individual but many people with differing gifts, callings, and ministries that accomplish the task.

That first summer we learned about teamwork. Either we did things together or somehow they didn't get done. Outspoken individualists caused rips in the personality fabric of the team. Like a glaring fluorescent-orange among the colors of the rainbow, a maverick just doesn't fit in the work of the body of Christ.

Leadership

That first summer Deyon and I learned how very important the issue of leadership is. The stark reality was that there were poor leaders on some teams and great leaders on other teams. And this marked the dividing line of blessing.

Character seemed to shine far above gifting or charisma. When times are tough, a leader with character can be trusted. Faced with the same difficulties, gifted individuals with weak characters become manipulators. And people get hurt.

A gifted director with character and natural charisma can lead a group of young mission candidates to walk on water, if necessary. And that illustrates one good test of leadership: Will the leader go in front?

Blessings of Difficulties

Mission candidates are often like semiprecious stones placed in a jar together with water and motion. The stones bump against each other, and rough edges are knocked away. As the operation continues, the beauty of the gems begins to delight everyone.

Difficulty is the gem-polisher. Unpleasant experiences always expose bad attitudes, selfishness, cultural bondages, intolerance, rigidity, and wrong presuppositions. Yet as we allow God to deal individually with us, His results begin to show loyalty, humility, willingness to follow, and the fruit of the Spirit.

Short-term mission experiences produce some beautiful jewels—individuals that truly radiate the message of Jesus. The process is often painful, yet few would forgo the experience. And after the initial tumbling, only gentle periodic polishing is required to restore the shining brilliance.

And so, for Deyon and me, that first summer set the course for the rest of our lives. These concepts we had learned would propel us through heavy seas. We would follow Jesus. He would lead us and always be with us. Difficulties and trials would always produce blessing as we followed Him.

It was that decision to "follow Him," made more than 20 years earlier, that brought us eventually to a ship called the Anastasis. It was that simple step of faith that led us to Greece. We could have never guessed back then that I would be directed into an Athens court to address a grim presiding judge.

CHAPTER
THREE

The Romanesque face of the presiding judge turned my way. For what seemed the longest of moments, he simply looked at me. *His mind is already made up*, I thought to myself as his cold gaze penetrated me. Then the translator explained that it was time for me to give my defense.

Throughout the day and the afternoon before, I had been turning a single question over and over in my mind. *What should I say?*

As I rose to my feet, I was the first of the three on trial to give a defense of our actions. And, to my surprise, I was quite calm. In the days preceding my testimony, several people had come to me with the promise found in Matthew 10:17-20:

> Be on your guard against men; they will hand you over to the local councils and flog you in their synagogues. On my account you will be brought before governors and kings as witnesses to them

31

and to the Gentiles. But when they arrest
you, do not worry about what to say or
how to say it. . .for it will not be you
speaking, but the spirit of your Father
speaking through you (NIV).

I knew the inner peace of the presence of the
Holy Spirit. Two things were highlighted in neon
lights from this passage in my memory. I was NOT
to worry about what to say and how to say it. We
biblical Christians should always tell the truth. The
truth is our only defense. It is not the delivery,
style, or language that gives power to any message,
either. Truth alone can penetrate like a razor edge
into the hardest of hearts.

A hush came over the courtroom. It seemed that
peace itself had somehow descended into that
crowded, active setting. Excitement began to stir
within me. Why were we on trial anyway? Was
it not an opportunity to tell others about Christ?

This would be my very first time to proclaim the
gospel in an actual court. Here were real, live
judges as well as onlookers, attorneys, praying
friends from almost every denomination in Greece,
and reporters from Athens' dailies and from the
Associated Press. There was drama, emotion, and
prison possibilities. It was all there.

Of course, I needed to face up to the fact that
a Simon Peter might reside just under my skin. I
had been following Jesus for some time before the
trial, but Peter and the 11 other apostles had lived
with Him daily for three years. They had listened
deeply as He tolu the parables. They had watched
with wide-open eyes as the blind were healed and

the lame walked. They had been the first to realize that Jesus was the promised Jewish Messiah.

Yet Peter didn't make it through the night when Jesus was arrested! Under the cross-examination of the authorities in Jerusalem, he lied, "I never knew him!"

If Peter, the great apostle, could so miserably yield to weakness, then it was surely possible for me to do so as well. And I didn't want some early-morning rooster reminding me of failure!

From deep within me came a request to God my Father. *Grant me boldness and wisdom,* I silently prayed. *May what I say be pleasing in Your sight. Someday I want to hear You say, "Well done, thou good and faithful servant."*

And so I began to tell my story. To the three judges and the rest of the audience I explained that our reason for being in Greece was a ship—a mercy ship. We had brought it to Greece to make some necessary alterations. We then intended to use it to help those less fortunate than ourselves.

On our ship there were 150 to 170 highly committed and loyal crew members with their families. Many of them were professional people who had volunteered one to three years or more to the mercy-ship project.

It was a dream that we all believed in completely. We had lost a similar dream once before, making this one even more precious.

After this introduction, I told the judge about Heidi and the gypsies.

The industrial community of Eleusis is about 40 minutes from Athens on the road to Corinth. While walking through the town with Deyon and the boys, Heidi, my eldest child, heard a pitiful cry. "What's that crying noise?" she asked her mother with alarm.

That section of Eleusis has several empty, abandoned storefronts. Some of the buildings are in a rather poor state of repair.

But where was the wail coming from? Heidi wound her way around the rundown structures and onto a small dirt pathway between two one-story store buildings. She pushed back some tattered blankets which had been hung to keep the January cold out of a small, two-room abode. There, on an earthen floor amidst a pile of blankets, lay a tiny baby. The cry grew louder, more insistent. A gypsy baby, just months old, and so hungry!

Nothing can touch the heart of a person more deeply than a needy child. Heidi hastily offered her allowance to purchase some yogurt and milk. Quickly the purchases were made. This practical assistance was gratefully received by the little gypsy family.

It didn't take long to discover that they also needed medical attention. Prayer was offered and plans puts into action. Others on the ship also had caring hearts and began to work with a number of other gypsies, who made up a considerable migrant population.

A South African family started regularly visiting them. Our chief medical officer, Dr. Doug Mar, provided medication and advice. Again I had been reminded of my mother's example: hearts and hands to help; prayers and practical helps; milk and medicine; Bibles and blessings.

Dr. Doug grew up in and around the church. But for him, like many second and third generations, a nominal relationship with God had crowded out the living faith of fathers and grandfathers. Dr. Doug knew much about God but did not really know Him at all.

Dr. Doug follow in his father's footsteps, excelling at academics. His bright mental capacity opened possibilities for medical school, and he enrolled. While doing his internship, a serious earthquake shook the Central American nation of Guatemala. Many organizations responded with material and medicine, and Dr. Doug went as a young intern.

The Ixil Indians were devastated in the quake. They had lost everything. Their homes lay strewn about the hillsides and the remains of their villages in piles of rubble. Almost everything came down about their heads. Everything was lost. Yet, they had something that the young American doctor did not.

For Dr. Doug, this encounter was the hand of Divine Providence. He had everything that modern society proclaimed was important. He was a young doctor in the United States, and a good salary and secure future awaited him. He would be able to purchase a nice home in the better subdivisions of American culture. He had it all just months before him, yet there was a great void within. A God-sized void that is in every living person. A void that only God can fill.

As he cared for the physical needs of the Ixils and administered the medical solutions to their wounds and diseases, he carefully studied their faces, and watched their responses. They really did have peace. It was well-water-deep within them, and tragedy did not cause it to run dry.

The two nurses invited Dr. Doug to accompany them to take photographs at sunrise, high on a hillside in the mountains of Guatemala. The brunette decided to stay at the foot of the hillside and pray. She knew her friend, the blonde, was going to ask Dr. Doug the most important question he would ever be asked.

They climbed the hillside, took their photographs, and sat down at the foot of the ten-foot-high cross that crowned the summit. They looked out over the desolation caused by the earthquake and thought of the Indians whose lives had been so drastically changed by it. Then Dr. Doug looked into the God-sized void in his own life.

The sun flooded across the sleeping valley. Shortly thereafter Dr. Doug asked for that void to be filled with the indwelling presence of Jesus Christ. Later with tears of joy, compassion, and gratitude, he would thank his Indian friends for what they had shown him. He had found the faith of his father. Education at Berkeley and medical school had not overwhelmed the influence of righteous roots.

It was accepting the challenge to live for God and not for self that eventually led him to marry one of the nurses. They joined the crew of the mercy ships.

Dr. Doug became a physician who brought not only physical help with one hand, but the hand of proclamation, telling about the Great Physician, with the other. Provision and proclamation. Physical and spiritual. Man is a whole being and all parts of him need ministry, not just the body.

Heidi and Dr. Doug, along with others from the mercy ship, had given gifts out of a heart of compassion. Little did they realize that an old law from an earlier dictatorship in Greece, the Metaxas regime, was lying on the legal books of that country.

If the law was dusted off and selectively applied (as it apparently had been over the last several years), then their acts of Christian charity could in fact be used against them and lead to criminal charges. Sound incredible? Yes, but sadly true.

An earthquake brought Dr. Doug to Christ. And an earthquake would bring me to trial.

During this time of helping the gypsies, our ship was docked in the quiet bay of Eleusis. These were pioneering days—we were birthing a new ministry! And as is normal in the early going of anything, we had to make do with what we had. We were like the early pioneers of the American West. Wagon experiences are bumpy, hot, uncomfortable, cold, mobile, man against the elements. That was a picture of the early days of the ship ministry.

I often compared the crew to the band that followed David before he was commissioned king. Someday they, too, would be like David's mighty men. Men and women who gained special honor because they joined their leader in his pioneering days and fought side-by-side with him.

Our support team members would join us later. Meanwhile we would do our best to follow God and to keep the work functioning efficiently.

Evening was the favorite time for many on board after a long, hard day at work: no noise; total quiet. A short distance away dozed the peaceful Greek countryside. There were no inner-city urban screams—just the lapping of waves as we rested at anchor in the peaceful Aegean Bay.

Suddenly, on February 24, 1981, at about 10:45 in the evening, an immense wave churned across the calm bay. It lifted our 11,695 gross registered tons high in the water and rolled us to starboard about 12 degrees. That would be nothing in a storm. But in a still, protected bay, it prompted us all to clamber out of our bunks. We rushed topside to see what had happened.

Speculations were flying. "Another ship must have hit us!" But there were no ships around. "It's some kind of a freak wave action!" But the Island of Salamis protected us from any such possibility. "Maybe a submarine crashed into us somewhere beneath the water!" None of these were true. Finally we all went to bed again, our questions unanswered.

At 4:55 in the morning a second wave rolled the ship to starboard. This time the officer on watch, Third Mate Bill Horn, heard women and children screaming on the island about half a mile off the ship's stern. He sounded the alarm. "Earthquake! It's an earthquake!"

The cries for help came from families whose cement and masonry houses were cracked or shattered by the seismic tremors. Our hearts were moved with compassion. To lose your house and possessions is a frightening thing! We quickly opened up the number one cargo hatch. Inside were many boxes of clothing donated by Christians in Athens. They had given the clothes as well as other materials thinking that they too could have a part in ministering to needy areas of the world.

Little did they know that their generous provisions would be distributed in their own surrounding villages and in parts of Athens itself!

As quickly as possible, Joe Portale organized the loading of the clothing, along with some emergency food items. We assembled technical, medical, and helping hands to go to the village of Perahora, the epicenter of the quake. We soon discovered that many villages had sustained damage.

The morning after the quake I had an appointment in Piraeus with a marine architect and a lawyer. Their seven-story office building was vacant. Many doors were standing open. Where was everyone? An abrupt tremor rattled through the building. I then realized why Piraeus had looked so deserted! I quickly descended the seven stories of stairs and joined everyone else outside the city.

That evening thousands of Athenians piled their families into their cars with a few precious possessions. They made their way to the seashore, where no skyscrapers could crash into them.

The undeveloped land surrounding both Piraeus and Athens looked like so many drive-in movie parking lots in North America. My heart went out to mothers, fathers, and children alike. I silently thanked God that we were on a ship, not in a cement building high in a city.

There was much to do. The Swiss Red Cross responded early with tents and blankets. We supplemented the effort with clothing and comfort. Fear and concern would wrinkle the brows of many fathers for days and weeks to come.

Their greatest fear was loss of loved ones.

Into these villages we took drama and outreach teams. Here was the second hand of the gospel—not only did we provide physical assistance, but now it was time for moral and spiritual help too.

An attorney friend, Mr. Odyseos, had lost everything in an earlier tragedy. He had lived in temporary housing, his home gone forever. He commented that more important than the soup, the blankets, and the clothing was the comfort given by loving, Christian people. It so warmed his heart and gave him the courage to start again. This was our goal.

Alan Williams was chaplain and evangelist for the ship. I was privileged to have him by my side. He had spent his early Christian years with Open Air Campaigners in New Zealand. It seems he just thrives on street meetings. And the greatest strength in Alan's life with Christ is prayer.

I well remember one occasion when we could not find him. We paged him on the ship's public address system. But we still could not locate him. Then finally we found Alan. He was sitting in the bottom of one of the cargo holds, pouring out his heart to God for the birthing of the ministry.

Alan organized the outreach teams from the ship which had been active in Greece since our arrival. We knew there were some peculiar laws on the books in Greece, but we really didn't think evangelism would be illegal. And now the earthquake focused our attention on the villages close to our shore accommodation.

Megara was the name of one picturesque village close by. Earthquake damage had been limited to a few houses, but all the villagers had felt the power of the seismic activity. In the center of the village was a typical Greek village square.

The shops surrounding it were whitewashed, just as their shopkeepers had kept them for centuries. The streets were regularly washed and swept.

Alan had the teams well-trained in drama and communication. Our purpose was to attract a crowd, much as the apostle Paul had done in his travels 19 centuries before. It was not unusual for several hundred people to gather and watch the presentation. By the time they left, they had heard the gospel.

The Greek villagers seemed to hunger for the message. The time was ripe for evangelism. But, according to Paul's writing to the church in Corinth, an open door brings many adversaries. And our adversary was just about to meet us.

Among the faces in the village throng, Alan saw a lone boy. This young man was accompanied by a handful of friends. But he seemed quite lonely and distressed. One of our crew, Dick Huizing, approached him.

Young Konstantine Koutopolon related the troubles that plagued his family. Communication had broken down between his parents. His mother had left home some years before and was now divorcing his father. It wasn't the earthquake that frightened him. It was, instead, the shattered relationship between his father and mother that had leveled the foundations of his family home. He didn't know if the marriage was repairable or if it had been permanently demolished.

Dick led 16-year-old Konstantine in a prayer. He asked God to make Himself known to Konstantine, to provide strength in the midst of family turmoil. He asked that each family member might find peace with God.

Konstantine had noticed the attractive New Testament offered by the outreach team. He requested one.

Konstantine was a bright lad. He spoke not only his native Greek but also English, French, and some German. Over the course of several weeks, Alan and several others prayed and counseled with Konstantine. They endeavored to provide him with stability and an environment for growth. Konstantine's father saw the positive effects of his son's association with the mercy ship crew.

His father brought him 12 to 14 times either to the ship or to our shore accommodations. Sometimes he remained with his son and enjoyed a meal with members of the crew. Other times he had business to attend to, so he left his son for a few hours.

Konstantine told us that the ship's families particularly impressed him. He saw mothers and fathers together with their children. It must have pained him to go home at night and have no mother waiting for him.

In the maritime profession, the family always suffers. Husbands are away for up to nine months at a time. Sailors are infamous for their activities in port cities of the world. The behavior of the Anastasis crew boldly contrasts with the lawless, harmful immorality that typically corrupts seamen. Many fine exceptions to this stereotype in the maritime field do exist, yet they too testify to the conditions of some of the ships' crews that call at various ports.

There are at least 50 children aboard ship. The "floating school" has an excellent teacher/pupil ratio of about one to eight. Education follows a British and American pattern. However, special attention is given to our Dutch families so their children can reenter the Dutch education system after their time aboard the mercy ship is complete.

One of the great attractions for biblical Christian seamen is the opportunity to follow their profession and not leave the family behind for extended periods. Deyon and I have lived aboard for several years with our four children. The experience of geography and world cultures has heightened our children's appetite for learning. We consider this unique education to be a great blessing. It is one of God's compensations for having no home besides the cabins on the ship.

Konstantine was in school himself during the week. His only time spent with us was on weekends. And we could see the boy transformed from one weekend to the next.

The more he read his Living Bible, the more he changed. God was working in his life! The pain began to leave his eyes. His smile brightened up. His father could see it also, and it caused him to encourage his son's visits.

Then the third seismic wave rocked our ship. But this one was man-made.

Konstantine's mother was enraged! She didn't want her ex-husband bringing her son to be with us. We found ourselves ensnarled in the heat of a domestic battle. At first we thought it was a tempest in a teacup. But a gale force wind was building up just beyond the horizon.

We had never met the mother. We didn't know where or with whom she lived. We didn't know why she was so angry. Was she full of bitterness at her husband, using her son as a hurtful tool to wound?

By now Konstantine's life had been radically altered. God had given him a new heart. Now he could love his mother even in the midst of her outbursts. He was embarrassed at her actions, but through counsel he saw that she needed him all the more. Prayer and hope were offered for an eventual reconciliation of the family. Unfortunately, that was not to be.

Mrs. Koutopolon, who has since changed her name to Mrs. Douka, filed for a restraining order. This would prohibit the father from bringing their son to see us. The order forbade his visits.

Alan went to Konstantine and explained the situation. "Please stay away," he instructed the boy. "Honor your mother even though it is extremely difficult. Pray for her relationship with your father. Perhaps you can help bring them back together."

"Is this the way Jesus would react, by sending me away?" Konstantine asked dejectedly. "Shouldn't I follow God and continue reading the Bible and spending time with other believers?"

Alan explained further. "The Bible clearly says to honor your father and mother—it's the first commandment with a promise. Konstantine, you must be willing to serve, to show by example the work of Christ in your life!"

In downtown Athens, a Christian man and his family held Monday evening meetings on Evripidou Street. This was not a church. It was simply a gathering place for Christian youth, and for those searching for reality in their lives. The mood was contemporary. The music was good. There was balance. And there was Bible teaching.

We hadn't wanted to leave Konstantine without any Christian fellowship. He would need mature Christians for counseling in the event of trouble. So, on a plain piece of paper, Alan wrote the name of the Athenian man and the address of his meetings.

> Costas Macris
> Youth Meetings
> Monday evenings
> Evripidou Street
> Athens

Alan and I never imagined that Costas Macris' name on that scrap of note paper would bring him to trial with the two of us. Three-and-a-half years later, the hastily scribbled name and address would be used as evidence against us all in an Athens court.

And 3½ years later Konstantine's mother would testify that the "Christians from the mercy ship" had ruined her son. "He doesn't get drunk like the other boys his age," she complained. "And he doesn't have a normal sex life."

I thought of my own children as she spoke. *So ruin them!* I prayed in my heart. *So ruin them, Lord Jesus!*

CHAPTER
FOUR

As the cross-examination of Konstantine's mother concluded, there was a brief delay in the proceedings. The earliest days of my marriage to Deyon began to come back to me. God had seen us through some incredibly difficult circumstances already, and He would guide this bizarre legal entanglement to its proper end as well.

Deyon and I were married in Grand Junction, Colorado. Grand Avenue took us across the Colorado river and into the National Monument with its towering red sandstone-sculptured pinnacles and perpendicular cliffs.

I so enjoyed the outdoors, and my beautiful home state.

To stand alone on a mountain ridge and look out upon the purple sage, the vast canyons, the snow-covered San Juan mountains with their caches of silver and gold, held an almost mystical power over me. I could almost sense the spirit of those early pioneers who had only partially tamed the land.

Those Western mountains teem with living
things. Majestic elk proliferate the high alpine
meadows. There they graze among columbine and
other delicate wildflowers. The graceful silhouettes
of mule deer can be discovered everywhere, as
well as the ubiquitous coyote, that mangy yet
brilliant scavenger. The yip, yip, yip of coyotes
howling at the moon, or the chorus of kits screaming like human babies, has put a healthy respect
for nature into many a lad.

Brown bear and mountain lion, locally known
as the cougar, also occasionally cross the Rocky
Mountain trails. A rare opportunity to watch a
mother bear and her cubs frolicking in the sun is
a treat not to be quickly bypassed.

My mountains! Their sheer magnificence
seduced me. Before I realized it, they became the
idol of my heart. I was guilty of worshiping the
creation more than the Creator.

Nevertheless, God was calling me to leave their
natural beauty. He had ordained one species more
valuable than all the rest. And it was God's love
for *man* that pulled most firmly at my heart.

Deyon and her family were well-established in
this city, but I was a relative newcomer. My
boyhood home was 50 miles away. Aware of my
commitment to serve God when my education was
completed, our pastor asked to talk to me.

He asked a number of questions about my
future. Pastor Schmidt was a wise, perceptive man,
and his love for the lost always moved my heart.
Somehow I wanted to model myself after him.
Here was a man who loved the outdoors but was
not bound by it. He worshiped the Creator more

than the creation. "God has a purpose for your life, Don," he encouraged me. "And it's going to take you far away from these red river valleys!"

He asked me to work with the church's young people. It was a large congregation—over a thousand attended on Sunday mornings. At that time it was the largest church in its denomination. Its influence was felt in business, in the local high schools, and in the community's athletic programs.

One of the chief reasons for this church's success was our pastor. He simply *loved* people. He exemplified God's love for man, revealing God's heart for everyone to see. I learned much from him. He believed in me and gave me opportunities to grow in service as well as faith.

While I studied at the college and worked as church youth leader, Deyon was busy completing her nurse's training. She was to become the "Outstanding Nurse of the Year" in the state of Colorado in 1965. We were both getting ready for our future mission service.

I had small conceptual struggles in finding a model for my chosen profession. The mission picture was rapidly changing. I somehow could not picture myself in white shorts and pith helmet in the heart of Africa. Nor could I picture myself standing in a pulpit Sunday after Sunday preaching to the same group of faithful people.

There had to be something else for me. I had a deep respect for those doing missions and pastoring, but I was struggling to find the exact trail that I was to follow. I began to take pilot's lessons. If Deyon was to be a nurse, then we both thought that I should be a pilot. That would add to our effectiveness in service.

When I was about 12 years old my mother had read to me a *Reader's Digest* feature selection about five young men who had given their lives among the Auca Indians in Ecuador. The words of Jim Elliot and the other four had become deeply imprinted on my young mind. Somehow I wanted to go replace them. With sincere boyishness I asked God to allow me to do something like that when I grew up.

Eventually I would stand on pier 53 in San Pedro beside the mercy ship. That had been the very pier that boarded Jim Elliot onto a ship bound for his destiny in Ecuador.

"He is no fool who gives what he cannot keep to gain what he cannot lose," Jim had once said.

Those words became another of God's markings on my soul. They bore deep into my heart and mind. Jim Elliot did not die in vain.

> Unless a grain of wheat falls into the ground and dies, it remains by itself alone; but if it dies, it bears much fruit (John 12:24 NASB).

My answer to the call to serve in Jesus' name was part of the fruitful harvest of Jim Elliot's life.

My burning desire was to be effective, and to someday hear my Father in heaven say He was pleased. So much of the world settles for second best, the mediocre. God wants us to do our best.

As weeks passed, Pastor Schmidt talked with me about the theological studies and education necessary for the ministry to which God was calling me.

We discussed several possibilities and had just about decided to head East. Then the president of Bethany Bible College spoke one Sunday morning.

After the service he talked to Deyon and me about his school in Santa Cruz, California. He interviewed us. He discussed us with our pastor. And he offered us a scholarship. Our decision was made!

Married just 3½ months, Deyon and I loaded the sum total of our possessions into a U-Haul trailer and headed West. We whispered goodbye to our glorious Rocky Mountains and drove through the "great empty quarter" of the American Southwest. From the Colorado border to Salt Lake City, the desert commands the landscape. Beautiful in a unique dimension, these barren brown hills seemed to be reminding us that we were leaving the blue-and-green high country for a long, long time.

Our delight knew no end as we came upon the verdant green of the Northern California coastline with its mighty redwoods. We were enchanted by Monterey Bay, Carmel-by-the-Sea, and historic old Santa Cruz with its century-old wooden wharf jutting out into the sea. Along the beach, surfers share the breakers with sea lions that inhabit the broken heads of Light House Point.

In spite of its lovely setting, Deyon almost cried as she viewed the empty, unfurnished, one-bedroom apartment that was to be our new home. It was musty with stale air. The carpets needed shampoo. We immediately set about making this place habitable.

Struggles to overcome disappointment would not

be unfamiliar in the years to come. Some of the places that eventually became "home" to us were to be far worse than that first California fourplex.

At Bethany College I enrolled in Greek, Old Testament Survey, Hermeneutics, and Psychology. I paid the president a visit to inquire about scholarships and a possible job. Both were available. I started immediately as a groundskeeper at the college.

My pastor had strongly encouraged beginning a ministry as soon as possible, and not making the mistake of thinking that ministry would always be in the future. So we contacted a small church in Felton, an old pioneer lumbering town picturesquely perched on the banks of the San Lorenzo River. A small church there hired us as assistant pastors while we studied. We gladly accepted.

I drove with Deyon to the Dominican Santa Cruz Hospital, where she applied for a job as a nurse. Upon being hired she learned that they were in the architectural stages of planning a new structure. Deyon and three other nurses were asked to travel to Stanford University for additonal classes in coronary nursing. They had been selected to assist in the new intensive care/coronary care unit of the soon-to-be-built hospital.

Several of Deyon's nursing friends were organizing a blood drive. The University of California at Santa Cruz had asked the Red Cross to enlist their student body to donate blood. I noticed that Bethany wasn't participating, so I suggested a competition between the two campuses. More than 200 pints of blood were collected from Bethany, just short of what was collected at the university campus!

Most of the 400 students at Bethany were studying to become proclaimers of the Word to a lost and dying world. The blood drive added substance to our message. Just as a spiritual revival had led to the founding of the Red Cross by Henri Du Gant, so our donation was a demonstration of loving Christian commitment to the hurting.

General William Booth, the founder of the Salvation Army, is often quoted: "A starving man cannot hear you preaching. Give him a bowl of soup and he will listen to every word." This must be true of the physically ailing too. The blood drive was another chapter in the two hands of the gospel—physical and spiritual. Meeting spiritual needs through practical means.

The class of 1969 elected me student body president. Four of us who were close friends were involved in student government—Al Akimoff, Joe Portale, Dave Boyd, and I.

During the course of a single week we all read a book that changed the course of our lives. It was Brother Andrew's *God's Smuggler*. That simple yet profound little tale explains how a single Dutchman obeyed God. It focused every one of us on a similar commitment.

Al Akimoff and I shared the experiences of our Caribbean summer with YWAM. Together we all discussed the possibility of joining Youth With A Mission after we graduated that May. It was like a people movement. From the Class of '69, the missions committee president, the student body vice-president, the class president, and a former class president all found ourselves going directly into missions overseas.

We were not joining some big, well-known, established group, but a very young mission with about 14 full-time staff members. There was no human reason for us to do this. In fact, many concerned friends counseled against it.

But our small "people movement" was convinced that we had heard that still, small voice. We believed that we were to be in the stream of Christian history and become change agents in foreign lands. Ambassadors among people who did not speak our language or think our thoughts. We were all young and quite inexperienced. Yet we knew that some kind of divine destiny lay directly ahead of us.

As graduation approached, we excitedly shared our goals. The mission's only center was in Switzerland. Did we have enough money to buy tickets to Europe? Which airline would we fly?

Someone discovered that Iceland had a national air carrier named Loftleider Airlines. This seemed to be the least expensive of all, so we agreed to meet in New York. God willing, we would all fly to Europe together.

We didn't have the money. I had been taking flying lessons and they had used what discretionary income we had. They were a great joy to me but also a temptation. And the call of the wild was still hidden in my bones. It nearly cost me everything before I ever got out of the U.S.A.

With great relish, I took a week off from my studies to drive back to Colorado with two friends for the autumn elk and deer hunt. The day before the season opened, we piled into Deyon's father's plane. Charlie Green was an excellent pilot with several thousand hours of mountain flying.

After taking off from Walter Field in Grand Junction, the 4900-foot elevation of the Grand Valley quickly dropped beneath us as the Cessna 182 gained altitude. We topped the red sandstone cliffs of the Colorado National Monument and moved on over Pinion Mesa.

After about 20 minutes of flying in the crisp October morning, we flew across the valley to the slopes of Grand Mesa. This flat-topped mountain has over 300 lakes on her slopes and thousands of deer. Large herds of elk also flourish there.

That's when the engine stopped.

"Something's wrong," Charlie said. "I've got full throttle and we've lost power." Earlier I had seen him go through the proper procedures to prevent carburetor ice. We were not in any position to cause a stall.

So why had the engine quit?

The glide ratio of a Cessna 182 is world-famous but not miraculous. With four grown men, full fuel tanks, and 10,000 feet of elevation, our plane would eventually and unavoidably come down!

Across the ravine, Charlie saw a small clearing among the quaking aspen trees. The clearing was only about 40 yards long and on an incline of about forty-five degrees. Unfortunately, it was our only hope.

The friend on my left had just caught sight of a large bull elk, the leader of a herd. It was a magnificent animal with its head high in the air,

almost challenging us to do battle for the suprem-
acy of the herd. My friend was so enthralled at the
beauty and size of the seven-point set of antlers
that he didn't even realize we were going down!

Meanwhile I was in the middle of my flying
lessons. Although I had only a few hours to my
credit, I had soloed. Now I watched with eyes wide
open. This was the real thing.

Charlie had the yoke full back, trying to slow
the 115-mile-an-hour plane before impact. His
hand was reaching across the cockpit to the right
for the electric flaps toggle switch. *Why do they put
it clear over there?* I wondered mutely.

My friend saw the tops of the trees going past
and called out, "Jesus, help us!" just at the moment of impact. The plane hit a large boulder in
the small clearing. The spring steel landing gear
was ripped off the plane. This kept us from cart-
wheeling into the trees. And it probably saved our
lives.

The plane split in half, the tail section winding
up 180 degrees from the nose of the aircraft.
Charlie turned around. His first act was to see if
we were all right. But his face was bloodied. It had
smashed into the instrument panel on impact.
Some 14 hours later he would require plastic
surgery—once we got to the hospital in the valley
below.

But miraculously we were all alive. I teased my
friend, "Do your praying *beforehand,* not *during* an
accident!" Because he had his mouth open praying, the impact had cracked several of his teeth.
Each time he took a breath, the exposed nerve
endings sent pain signals of high intensity to his

brain cells. He was soon in shock. At the time I didn't realize he was so badly hurt.

After four hours of negotiating mountain trails on a badly damaged left ankle, I arrived at a rural utility station. No one was there. Nevertheless, I entered and telephoned for assistance.

Two years later Charlie received a commendation for outstanding piloting of the little plane. In the meantime, the Federal Aviation Administration had recalled all models of that particular aircraft. They had discovered a part in the carburetor that was susceptible to metal fatigue after a certain number of hours. That very piece of metal had broken and caused our motor to stop!

Once back in Santa Cruz, my flight instructor there insisted that I get right back into a plane and fly it myself. Had he not pushed me, I could quite possibly have succumbed to a permanent fear of flying. His encouragement and belief in me helped me overcome a major obstacle.

Meanwhile, Deyon and I still needed the finances to join our friends in Europe. One disappointment loomed ahead of us. We had expected the finances to come from our church. But word arrived that since the mission was interdenominational, we would receive no financial assistance.

Brother Andrew in his book *God's Smuggler* had spoken of God always making a way, the "Royal Way," when we trust in the King. And at this point we had no alternative. Trust was all we could do!

The day before she was to leave her job at the Dominican Santa Cruz hospital, Deyon picked me up from work. She had a radiant smile and a twinkle in her eyes. Something amazing had happened. And it *had* to be an answer to our prayers.

The Bishop of the Monterey Diocese of the Catholic Church was in the intensive care/coronary care ward at the hospital. In talking to Deyon, he had begun asking many questions. He found out that we were shortly to head for Europe. And he politely inquired about our finances.

Deyon tactfully explained that our church would not assist because of the interdenominational aspect of the young mission. "Then," said the Bishop, "perhaps my church could help!"

I listened to her story with some skepticism. Could it be possible that when our own church could not help us, the Catholic Church would be willing?

The next day the Bishop handed Deyon an envelope with 200 dollars in it. "Here, Deyon," he smiled. "God bless you. Use this wisely, now!"

When she arrived home, we bowed our heads and thanked God for His remarkable answer. Then a little later our church gave us an offering and commissioned us into missionary service.

On Sunday I found a classified advertisement for a newly painted and overhauled 1963 Ford pickup truck. I telephoned for information. It could be our transportation to Colorado. There we would store our wedding gifts and my library.

The voice on the other end of the phone sounded open and warm. He asked a few penetrating questions. It seemed he knew my name—he had met me once before. He was a deacon in a Conservative Baptist church in the Santa Cruz area.

The deacon said that he and his wife often gave

to missions, and that they would be delighted to help us on our way toward Europe. He reduced the price of the pickup to a token amount. "Whatever you get from the sale of it is my investment in the kingdom of God through your lives!" That investment turned out to be over a thousand dollars.

Finally we were ready. Our bags were packed. Our hands clutched one-way tickets to Luxembourg. We had no promised monthly support, but our hearts and hands were eager to help others. Al Akimoff, Joe and Judy Portale, Dave and Carol Boyd, Deyon and I—we were all on our way!

We were young, vigorous, and adventurous. We had a call from God on our hearts. We said goodbye to family and friends. Our churches had sent us off; they probably had some misgivings, but they trusted God enough to send us in His care.

We had no concept of the momentous things that God would place before each of us.

Soon we would learn different languages, and answer different callings, yet all from the same God. We would learn, in time, the magnitude of God's work in the world.

I would eventually sit soberly in an Athenian trial, where my future would rest in the hands of the King of Kings Himself. But hadn't it always been there?

CHAPTER
FIVE

Despite the humorless atmosphere of the courtroom, I couldn't help but smile a little, remembering that first flight overseas. The seven of us had
gathered at JFK airport, and what an amusing sight!
Our zeal and excitement were evident, but it was
also readily obvious that we were novices when
it came to world travel.

Of course we all hoped to share our faith with
fellow passengers. But beyond that opportunity,
we really weren't certain what we were getting
into. The mission was very young, with no proper-
ties and no established track record. But what a
great dream—the dream of reaching our generation for Christ!

And if the mission was young, we were even
more so. It is difficult to appear sophisticated
during one's first or second venture outside his
own country!

Joe Portale had a fast-growing beard. As a pre-
caution to 5 o'clock shadow, he had placed two

giant shaving cream cans in the liner of his winter coat. And that wasn't all he had stashed there, either. He looked like he was headed for Siberia!

Fortunately, airplane hijacking had not yet been introduced to the world. Joe would have sent one of today's metal detectors into orbit with all the metal stashed in his coat lining. One could only wonder how he would fare in the suave French culture to which God was calling him!

Joe and Judy would study French in Lausanne at the Ecole Lemania. They would eventually join forces with others in Lausanne. There they would see God bring into existence a work where nothing had been done before.

The strategy was to build up strong relationships with the pastors of local churches, to serve them in evangelism and in training. To do this, one must immerse himself totally in the provincial culture. Joe, with his European heritage, was an ideal candidate for this work.

Al Akimoff was one of Joe's closest friends. He would find his way to Austria where God would allow him to establish a center from which he would send teams into the Soviet Union, one of the last truly unreached areas of the world. Al's Russian background gave him a strong, warm heart for a unique, demanding ministry.

David and Carol Boyd joined Deyon and me as we headed for Germany. German families housed us, transported us, prayed with us, and believed in us. I spoke no German, but only for a few days. Then Karl-Heiz Leinberger (who spoke no English) and I began to converse together. Our dialogue was alternately animated, hilarious, and serious.

Word-by-word, day-by-day, we began to understand the culture.

We gathered together with the Boyds, the Braggs, and Deyon's brother, Lynn, and headed for Berlin. We would attend language school at the well-established Goethe Institute on Knesebeckstrasse 31.

On the way we passed the Kaiser Wilhelm Gedekneskirche, the bombed-out structure left as a memorial to the ravages of war. In later years we would often gather on the steps of that church to converse with scores of disillusioned youth. There we would quietly endeavor to answer their questions, the same questions that were being asked on so many university campuses worldwide.

Why war? Why do the innocent suffer? Where was God in World War II?

One of those inquiring young men, Mounir, was an exchange student in East Berlin. The East German government had financed his university studies. Out of curiosity he decided to cross at Checkpoint Charlie into the western sector of the divided city for a weekend.

Mounir saw unprecedented dedication in the lives of the ones witnessing. Eventually he left his university studies in East Berlin. He accepted the challenge of YWAM and went on to lead a large segment of the organization's work in the Middle East.

One bitterly cold October afternoon, Deyon and I boarded the U-bahn to travel toward the home of a German pastor. He had graciously provided us with a place to stay. The German pastor and his Swiss wife were responsible for three congregations in West Berlin.

We got out of the U-bahn in Wedding, near the Berlin Wall—one of the poorer sections of the city. As we made our way up the steps that led out of the subway, a peculiar sound filled our ears. It was the tremendous roar of thousands of people shouting in unison, combined with the thunder of marching feet.

At the end of the street, the infamous Wall glared at us. It is like a painful scar dividing the historic and powerful old city. As we walked up the street toward our friends' apartment, we could see the pockmarks on the facia of the stone and masonry buildings. Bullet scars were still clearly visible almost 25 years after Hitler's fall.

The heavy wooden doors that we passed bore marks left by Russian troops as they came to "liberate" this section of Germany. Oak door after oak door had felt the violent impact of Russian marching boots as they were kicked in during search-and-seizure procedures.

But what was the awesome sound that deafened us to all else? The wall was getting closer; the noise was getting louder. Cold tentacles of fear gripped us. We had to work at not wishing ourselves thousands of miles away!

In the safety of the pastor's apartment, we listened as a radio announcer explained the volume of noise penetrating the entire building. It was a large, carefully planned celebration of the infamous October revolution of 1917.

I had an urge to see this demonstration. It was all so foreign to the system of liberty and freedom that I loved. My brother-in-law, Lynn, met me in the U-bahn, and together we exited West Berlin at Karl Marx Allee. We went up onto Karl Marx Platz. There we encountered tens of thousands of young people. They marched because they had been told to march!

Lynn and I quickly dived in, although the bright green windbreaker I was wearing did not exactly match the colors of the rest of the huge throng. We were told that 350,000 young people were marching to celebrate the overthrow of capitalism.

The obvious lack of joy and enthusiasm made a deep impression on our minds: regimentation; stifling of personal freedoms; forced marching; no spontaneity. It didn't seem like a celebration or an occasion that the marchers would even want to remember. The hollow emptiness in their eyes was to stab again and again into my memory. It so clearly reflected the bondage of antichristian philosophy and the politics of power. As I contemplated this, a vision began to grow within my heart and mind. Why not show the world the difference?

What if thousands of biblical Christians, rich in the joy of redemption and forgiveness, were to march? What if they were to march into the cities of the world? There would be music, truth, and drama. It would be a true celebration and a glorious witness. To know Christ is to have a real cause to celebrate.

This very vision was the beginning of YWAM's large international outreaches. At places like the Olympic Games, we learned to impact the whole world in microcosm. And the surprising genesis of all this was in East Germany—amidst 350,000 marching Communist youth.

By the time the 1972 Munich Olympiad rolled around, over a thousand Christians from 52 different nations would be living in a sixteenth-century Bavarian castle. And their purpose would simply be to minister to the Olympic athletes and visitors.

The organization of such an effort requires masses of advance prayer and planning. To prepare for this kind of endeavor, a trio was sent to Bavaria and the Olympic city of Munich. They were to do feasibility studies and research.

The trio included Doug Sparks plus my brother and sister-in-law, Gary and Helen Stephens. Doug and Gary had known each other for years, having grown up in the same rugged Colorado mountains.

Gary phoned one day, excitedly explaining that a sixteenth-century Bavarian castle had been located for accommodations. I almost missed the Lord here! I was thinking of something a bit more conservative than a castle.

Deyon and I knelt in our room there in Chalet-a-Gobet, on the outskirts of Lausanne. We earnestly began to seek God in prayer. Could it be right for the mission to buy such a unique structure?

We called Joy Dawson to pray with us. God always seemed to arrange for Joy to be with us when we faced important decisions. We had observed her persistent searching of the Scriptures in her desire to learn of His character and ways. She is a straight arrow. There is no lightness in her approach to the business of building God's kingdom.

After much prayer, we believed the Lord was

saying yes. I went to a bank in downtown Lausanne to begin discussions about finances and legalities. What would it require to accomplish such a purchase? I had long felt we should begin a mission work in Germany. Perhaps this was the opportunity.

I telephoned Loren the next day. We agreed to meet and take a look at the castle. If it was satisfactory, we would negotiate and attempt to buy it. As it turned out, the castle was given by God to the mission! And it became our home until God called us back to Switzerland.

The second week of the Olympics shocked the world to a standstill. It was the birth, a gruesome birth, of international terrorism. It burst smack into the center of a peaceful sporting event. I was listening to a radio in the castle when the horrifying news bulletin broke through the regular programming:

ARAB TERRORISTS HAVE MURDERED SEVERAL ISRAELI OLYMPIC ATHLETES. WE'LL BROADCAST MORE DETAILS AS SOON AS THEY ARE AVAILABLE.

My heart stopped. I was gripped with sorrow. I rushed out to the nearest vehicle and found my way to Munich, where I gathered our outreach teams. More than 70 of us sadly bowed our heads in prayer just outside the Olympic Athletes Village. "O God!" we cried. "Help our hurting world . . . send peace . . . use this evil act of murder to turn man's eyes toward You . . . toward peace."

We were seeing a repeat performance of the way

the 1938 Berlin Olympics were opportunistically used by Hitler. He had politicized the games for his own purposes. Now Haus 37 in the Olympic Village was center stage worldwide. International television had most of the world glued to their sets in suspense.

Hundreds had attended the Olympics for peaceful reasons. They sat in mourners' circles on the cobblestone pathways. They wept in identification, and gave moral support. The mayor of Munich contacted the committee of Christian organizations, some 67 all told, with a simple request.

"There is so much sorrow and division now. Our city and nation wanted so much to show the world that there was another side to Germany, beyond the specter of Hitler. But now violence has again come to Munich. Could you arrange for thousands of youth to hold a peace march through the center of the city?"

Munich opened her Municipal Gardens and provided 30,000 flowers for us to distribute free of charge. Along with each blossom a tract was given explaining that peace comes only through forgiveness, and not by violence. We gathered outside the ancient city walls at Brandenburger Tor. The march began.

It wasn't the only march taking place in Munich. But it was certainly unique and peaceful. Thousands of people received literature, and those who read it were faced with the reality that one could find peace only through God.

One young lady, a resident of Israel, led an Arab into a relationship with Jesus, the Jewish Messiah. Newspapers carried the photo the next day. How beautifully it portrayed the stark difference between the philosophy of violence and the message of Christ to love our enemies.

Among the 67 Christian organizations and denominations there in Munich the unity was so strong that it could almost be touched. For months after the march, letters would come in from all around the globe. These messages related individual stories: "Someone prayed with me" or "I was given a tract." The Y.M.C.A. in Munich was a wise, guiding hand in all of the events both before, after, and during the followup. A thriving church had its beginnings in the witness of 1972. In this way the outreach continued on and on.

But it was just the beginning of God's fulfillment of the vision I had glimpsed that October day in East Berlin. And the passage in Isaiah 11:9 was lodged in my mind. Would it be fulfilled in my lifetime? Would I be able to participate?

> The earth will be full of the knowledge
> of the Lord as the waters cover the sea
> (NIV).

A castle in Bavaria is a long way from an apartment in California! We had made the floor beneath the east turret into offices and living quarters. I was enjoying the challenge of taking the aftermath of an international event and turning it into something national and long-term. But there was a loneliness in my heart. I missed my mom and dad, my friends, and my beloved mountains. Now I was learning that to follow Christ means to continually give up to Him anything that would keep me from total obedience. As I dealt with these things, the Scripture from Mark 10:28-31 came to mind:

> Peter said to him, "We have left every-thing to follow you!" "I tell you the truth," Jesus replied, "No one who has left home or brothers or sisters or mother or father or children or fields for me and the gospel will fail to receive a hundred times as much in this present age (homes, brothers, sisters, mothers, children and fields—and with them, persecutions) and in the age to come, eternal life. But many who are first will be last, and the last first" (NIV).

God was calling us on.

The mission in Germany would be left in the very capable hands of our friends Dave and Carol Boyd. Soon many others would join them. And one couple in particular, Keith and Marion Warrington from New Zealand, would totally immerse them-selves in the culture.

Meanwhile, Deyon and I had been in the Middle East for three months. There we had led about 140 young people on a practical evangelism field trip. We had learned from Loren Cunningham. Now we were following his model.

In Greece we boarded a ship bound for Haifa. The captain graciously allowed me to go up to the bridge and observe the officer of the watch as he navigated the blue Mediterranean Sea.

On the return voyage I peeked into the engine room. The many motors and the maze of pipes overwhelmed me. I gained new appreciation for the engineers who run those big ships. Never in a thousand years would I have guessed that I would eventually become a maritime missionary!

At this time Deyon was expecting our second child. Little Heidi had been born three years earlier in Lausanne. She had grown rapidly accustomed to the German culture, looking very much the part with her light blond hair and sparkling blue eyes.

During a stopover in Lausanne, Deyon was required by the doctor to spend the remaining four months of her pregnancy in bed. The doctor was concerned that we might lose the child if she didn't. This posed a dilemma for us as a family. What should we do? Since Loren Cunningham and I would both be traveling, Deyon would move in with Darlene there in Lausanne. I would come back as often as possible.

But by April 1974 Loren and Darlene had packed everything up and headed toward the Pacific and Asia following a six-month stay in Los Angeles. This meant that the responsibility for Europe, the Middle East, and Africa now rested heavily on my shoulders. This was more than a job. Our closest family friends were serving in those various countries. Our interest in that work was deep and personal.

In Switzerland I was also faced with the task of trying to learn the French language. German had been difficult, though not impossible. But French— my tongue just didn't seem to have the capacity to pronounce the words. Worse yet, Deyon was well ahead of me. That did nothing for my male ego.

Heidi and Luke spoke with the local Vaudois

accents. They were mildly embarrassed at Father's Yankee pronunciation. Nevertheless, we began to speak French at home. Several of our French-speaking friends were quite tolerant. Others politely elected to converse in English. I was never sure if they were trying to improve their English or to save us all the embarrassment of my poor French!

For Deyon and me, the six years we lived in Lausanne were among our very happiest. It was there that we began to really learn the ways of God. It was there that a number of our deepest friendships were forged through hardship and victory. It was there that many of YWAM's European, Middle East, and African works were birthed.

In Lausanne, a former orphanage and farm, Burtigny, was given free of charge to the mission. And in Lausanne a powerful video and cassette ministry began.

But somehow the city of Amsterdam was on my heart. I needed to be there in the summer of 1973. And I sensed that God had a new and interesting turn in the road for me and my family.

The two hands of the gospel, practical and spiritual, were not really being used in my ministry. I felt that something was missing. I had done a lot of evangelistic proclamation, and I had loved doing it, but the Holy Spirit was tugging at something deeper.

Was it boats or ships? In Amsterdam, that city of canals and rivers, God would begin to stir my interest in the use of vessels for ministry. And Amsterdam would eventually lead me to Athens.

CHAPTER SIX

The Athens courtroom seemed distant and detached from all that was so precious. Loneliness crept momentarily into my thoughts. Yes, Alan and Costas were on either side of me on the defendants' bench. Yet each of us was alone with his thoughts.

Once again the piercing gaze of the presiding judge met my eyes. Would he see my honesty? Did he realize that we were not criminals? Was he aware that this wasn't the first time in history that the Book had been fought over? Did he know that God's Book couldn't be stopped? Could he, like Agrippa who heard Paul's case, be "almost persuaded" to be a believer himself?

He asked me a pointed question.

"Why were you in Greece in 1981? What were you doing here?"

From deep within me swelled a wellspring of courage. Our dream was on trial! The dream was really not mine or ours, for it originated in the compassionate heart of God. And our dream was good. It would enable us to use two hands to proclaim the gospel of peace.

"Your Honor, with all due respect, I'm here because of a dream of doing good. I want to help others to provide hearts and hands to help. Our dream has to do with a ship. The name of the ship is Anastasis, Greek for resurrection. We lost our dream once, and this is its rebirth.

"We purchased a rather large passenger/cargo ship in Italy and brought it here to Greece to retrofit the vessel. That is why I was in Greece, sir."

My mind quickly flashed back to the very beginning of our maritime ministry. Each small river tugboat left its own quiet wake as it did its part in towing two massive houseboats through a maze of Dutch canals.

Up until now one of the boats had served as a school for the Rhine River's boat children. The other boat had been a dormitory for lodging and meals. Now the destination of these tugs and boats was the city center in Amsterdam.

Because of the height of one of the boats, a rather circuitous route was required to bring them to their final mooring just behind the Central Train Station in downtown Amsterdam. The Havengebouw, which houses the harbor authorities, hovered like a towering guardian angel, overlooking the boats' slow progress.

It was hoped that these vessels still had 15 years of life left in their hulls. At the time that was questionable. Yet in the next decade-and-a-half, people without number would make their peace with

God somewhere on board. Like Francis Schaeffer's famous Swiss haven for intellectuals, these boats became a sort of floating retreat. Here the searching youth of Europe, often headed for India's pagan mysticism, were invited to stop and hear the truth of God.

One vessel was named the Ark, the other later renamed Dilaram, a Persian word meaning peaceful heart. They soon heard the feet of many nations cross their decks. Laughter and the probing questions of brilliant, searching minds would resound within their hulls.

I had originally intended to spend only a summer in Amsterdam, but the city gripped my heart. There were thousands of aimless young people in the streets. There was an immense drug problem. Surely God had led us to the very heart of Holland's most famous city for more than three short months!

That summer we did something rather unusual: We joined with other pastors in the city to pray and walk. For six weeks we prayed and walked the Amsterdam avenues. One hundred and twenty people, from more than a dozen nations, gathered together to pray for the people of Amsterdam.

We joined in with city people as well as with people from the countryside. Together we prayed for God to establish a work. The city was divided into a systematic pattern. Each major section was covered by long lines of Christians walking two-by-two, lifting the lost before the Lord.

At the close of this time of intercession, we rented a ballroom in the Krasnipolsky Hotel on the Dam Square. A newly converted couple,

horticulturists who wanted to give a gift of gratitude to the Lord and also to Amsterdam, provided
10,000 long-stemmed red roses.

We walked again through the city streets. We
now had God's heart for these people. With deep
joy we handed each person a red rose and a piece
of literature.

I can still see the puzzled face of one elderly man.
Had no one ever before given him a rose? "Why
me?" were his words.

His penetrating eyes seemed to probe my mo-
tives. Didn't the most beloved of all flowers, the
rose, signify something special? Only for memorial
occasions did one give roses. They shouldn't be
handed out to strangers! "Why me?"

Why *not* him? Was he unaware that Someone
had given him, even though a total stranger, a far
more valuable gift? Ten thousand roses are costly
indeed. But think of it—what did our eternal life
cost Jesus?

I had spent the summer on the two boats. Now
at the conclusion of our prayer-in-the-streets cam-
paign, I pondered the future. I knew the principle: God won't release something to you unless
you are prepared to pay the price. I had faced that
fact before we ever placed a down payment on the
boats. Yes, I was prepared to live in Amsterdam.
In fact, I quite enjoyed the Dutch and their open,
frank mannerisms.

But there was a far deeper struggle going on. The
mission was in its Gethsemane. Loren Cunningham was convinced that now was the time for us
to purchase a ship.

I watched the ships ply the harbor. I took the

canal cruise more times than I care to remember. Something was happening in my heart about ships—no doubt about that. Here I had a growing interest in using ships to minister the gospel with both hands. And YWAM was in the midst of trying to purchase a vessel in faraway New Zealand. But something didn't seem right.

I had watched and participated with all my heart as the work grew. Loren's dream had become our own dream too. Many of us were doing everything possible to fulfill that dream of reaching our generation with the gospel.

But the ship was another matter. How do you tell your leader that something isn't right? It wasn't the idea of purchasing a ship that bothered me. We all believed in that. It just seemed too much for us to tackle right then.

Loren came to see Deyon and me on his way to a Scandinavian conference. As I helped him drive the Land Rover that pulled his trailer, we talked over many things—the financial needs at the castle, offerings for the ship, the outreach in Amsterdam.

At one point I tried to say something about the timing of the ship purchase, but I didn't want to cause a distance between us or to imply that we weren't supporting him. He had supported me so often. Still, the sinking feeling would not go away.

Weeks later found me on my way to a conference in Japan. The time there was a watershed for me and the mission.

Several people had come solely because of the ship. But it was in Osaka, at the Youth Hostel, that God showed us His mind. There wouldn't be a ship right then!

In the time of disappointment that followed this realization, I became deeply and personally convicted of sin. There in Osaka I stood on my feet and wept. God was showing me the bottom of my heart. I found two trustworthy, mature friends and confessed things privately. I knew the power of cleansing. And I wanted to be truly known—not to have secrets to take to my grave.

To be known. To have nothing to hide. God has called us to be living epistles, known and read by men. Only through confession can this happen. It is by way of confession that we find freedom in Christ.

The way God pictured it for me was in the drawing of a heart. The top was clean. But down in the very bottom were two or three things with which I continually struggled. It was as though the enemy had a hook in me there. Those particular sins gave him a platform in my life from which to wage war on me. It was these things that I confessed to God before my friends and asked them to pray for me.

In Japan I found victory. I was free. I was bruised by the hand of God in soul surgery, but free. Of course it didn't mean that I would never sin again. But I had painfully learned to humble myself before God and man.

These Osaka meetings lasted just less than two weeks. On many days we didn't have teaching. Instead we read from the Book and spent hours on our knees. It marked me. It marked the mission.

Yes, we would lose the ship. Financial complications prevented us from concluding our contract. But we wouldn't lose the most valuable thing of all: our relationship with God. The loss of the ship and its 72,000-dollar deposit became a "cross" in the mission. In each of us, individually and corporately, there is much that must die. And death is never pleasant.

Almost a year later, the mission leaders met at a desert retreat. There Loren did a most difficult thing. I watched him walk to the podium. As he ascended the three steps, his shoulders drooped. The spring in his step was gone. We watched in rapt attention. Humbly he started to speak about the loss of the ship. But he could not go on. The words somehow would not come. He seemed to crumble under the weight of having disappointed all of us, of having disappointed the Lord.

Then, spontaneously, from all around the building, young men rose to their feet. They silently stood, wordlessly identifying with him. I decided, then and there, that it would be a privilege to follow this man around the world. This was reality—no cover-up. Here was God's army, wounded, having lost a battle and suffered embarrassment. But there were no empty words, no excuses. Our failure was exposed for all the world to see.

God allowed us to lose. Yet He also gave us a will to win. Someday He would give us a resurrection. As in the Bible, many of God's promises are conditional. There would be guidelines for us to follow. But years later, resurrection would come.

Ten years later I boarded the London-to-Venice train as it passed through Lausanne.

Floyd McClung, Lynn Green, Jeff Fountain, Mark Spengler, and a couple of others joined me there. We were going to inspect a ship called the

Victoria. Together we traveled to Mestre, the last stop before going on to the Island station in Venice. We had rooms in the Plaza Hotel just across from the station.

After strategizing and talking for several hours on the train, we all headed for our beds with their welcoming down comforters. On my bed, alone with my thoughts, I went over my recent telephone call with Loren. I had explained everything to him. God was stirring in my heart! And the stirring had to do with the release of the ship.

Why had God been stirring me? Shouldn't Loren be the one? What was my role? Why me? Those questions rolled over and over in my mind.

Loren had been quiet on the transcontinental phone call. I sensed his struggles and prayed quietly for him. We had already discussed it with him and several other people on YWAM's International Council. Prayerfully we had evaluated the possibilities. Now it was time to pursue the ship. But the fear of God was on me. To even think of taking on the project after our previous disappointment was unnerving.

After a continental breakfast in the hotel dining room, our team gathered in my room for a time of prayer. Unspoken in each of our thoughts was the fact that we had lost one ship. This transaction had to be handled properly! Yet we were so inexperienced, so aware of our need of God.

That morning our praise had a mighty ring to it. Singing in spiritual warfare had become extremely meaningful, and our fervent prayers earnestly invoked God's assistance. How clearly we identified with young King David as he faced his giant with only a sling and stones.

We had even less! This dream was a giant. It would either make men of God out of us, or slay us. Worse yet, it could destroy the mission. What a big risk we were taking!

I silently thanked God for a mission that was willing to take risks—calculated, prayerful, feasible risks, yet without God—impossible risks. Doubt raised its ugly head every time one of us strayed from the promise and ability of God to accomplish the task. We couldn't. He could.

We boarded the train again for the seven-minute ride to Venice.

As we approached the station, off to our right loomed a big white ship. Surely that couldn't be the Victoria! Our hearts sank.

We met with the representatives of the Adriatic Company, a state-controlled organization. They had chosen to modernize their fleet. All passenger ships were being sold.

After some discussion, we made arrangements to board the vessel and have a look around. There were four watchkeepers and one officer on board. They had already run the generators for half an hour that morning, and now they were shut down. We would have to tour cold insides of the ship in the dark.

The Victoria was designed to carry 674 crew members and passengers. She could also handle 4000 tons of cargo. She was immense. And the further we went down the darkened hallways with our flashlights, the faster the faith of the morning's prayer meeting ebbed from our hearts.

Surely God wouldn't want us to buy this ship. She was too big. Too dark. Too much work.

My brother-in-law, Lynn Green, ever the curious one, found his way down into the bottom of hold number three. There on the bulkhead, in the bowels of the ship, he played his flashlight. The bright beam showed a watermark. It ran from low in one corner at a 35-degree angle toward the upper deckhead on the opposite side.

The ship must have rolled mightily in some storm. At the sight of the evidence, my heart was in my shoes. I could get seasick just walking on the wooden wharf in Santa Cruz! In Colorado, terra firma was granite, rock solid beneath my feet. What would I ever do in a storm at sea?

We spent several hours poring over most of the ship. It was clear to us that we needed to hire the best professional marine consulting agency that we could find. We needed an outside, independent study. Another mission had already evaluated the vessel and we had their paperwork, but we were novices, and we thought it wise to spend the extra money for a second opinion. Three Quays Marine Services, Ltd., a subdivision of Lloyd's, flew to Venice from London to survey the ship.

Basically the hull and machinery were sound. She was an old ship, with her keel first laid in 1953, but she was sound. With tender loving care, hard work, and time, she could once again be made almost new.

Despite my fears, I could picture the dream birthed in God's own heart for a mission ship. A mercy ship. A salvation ship. A battleship. A training ship. A hospital ship similar to the former S.S. Hope, but dedicated to God.

Our ship would sail the seas with hundreds on board from many nations. We would plant churches, build schools, establish refugee camps, feed the hungry, and rescue the perishing. Some would weep as they went sowing the seed. Others would rejoice as they brought in the harvest. All of this would be accomplished with the two hands of the gospel, in the name of Jesus.

But the ship was still not ours. We were still not certain that this was the one. The feasibility studies were all in. It looked as if she would be economical to use once we were underway. In fact the figures clearly showed us that the Victoria would require the same operating expense budget as our land centers in Europe or America.

I called the leadership team together in Lausanne. In the beautiful forest just behind my rented home we talked and prayed. For several years I had served these men, mostly my age, as the director of YWAM for this region of the world. They were my closest friends. They were spending valuable time away from their own mission responsibilities in various countries. We were in this together and unless we had unity, we would not go on. We began to pray, seeking God for permission to buy a smaller ship. There were several others for sale. We had seen three sister ships that weighed only about 2000 tons each, a sixth of the Victoria's almost 12,000 tons. These vessels could carry only about a quarter as much material and people, but the size looked much better to most of us.

Then one of the others prayed the prayer that

exposed my own heart. I heard him say, "Father, let us have but one of those smaller ships; we can do that for You. This one is too big. We cannot do it."

Like a tree crashing in the forest around us, understanding broke through to me. Of course! We had been looking at it from man's perspective. *But if we could do it, then we didn't need God.* How wrong of us, to think that we could do it for Him! He was allowing us the privilege of cooperating with Him in His dream.

He would do it; we would help. He would teach us; we would be His students. Our responsibility was to obey Him. To follow Him. To serve Him and to serve others. Yes, we would buy the big white ship.

But we didn't have the money.

How could we approach people with a project this size when they probably knew we had failed before? The last time God wouldn't let us borrow the money. This time it seemed that we must. If we were not sure enough of this dream, then we would not be able to convince others.

We took out mortgages on our existing centers. In Switzerland we borrowed in Swiss francs to buy a ship with American dollars. The same in Germany, Holland, and England. This was during the time of the dollar's all-time low. Little did we know that currency markets would reverse, and we would soon have almost a million dollars at a negative interest rate.

This was to be God's ship entrusted to the mission, not just my project to develop—so each national council discussed and prayed about the plan separately. Many of the mission staff made monthly pledges, even though they received only paltry monthly support themselves. Their standing with us still causes emotion to well up in my heart. It was true commitment. Everyone bought in.

The ship was still not ours.

We had nine months to come up with the money. Mark Spengler and I traveled to Rome to meet with the Minister of Maritime Affairs, a cabinet-level official in the Italian government.

This kind, elderly gentleman listened to our dilemma and our projected use of the ship. When he found that it was not for commercial usage but to be a mercy ship, he phoned through to the company director in Venice.

"Hold the ship until the mission can get all the money together. Keep it for them and sell it to them at the scrap value."

He looked at us carefully. He commended us on what we were doing. He said the world needed more people doing what we were doing, and perhaps someday it would be a better world. Then he told us that he was a believer. "Someday I'll stand before God. I want to have some part in this ship too."

How I thanked God for this man! He believed in us and what we were trying to do. That gave us courage and the will to go on.

Meanwhile a Dutch shipowner drove down to Venice from Holland in his Mercedes. He toured the ship from stem to stern, top to bottom, and spent quite a bit of time in the engine room. Together we looked the ship over for wasted metal or weaknesses. He and his brothers operated ships from Delfzijl in the north of Holland. His advice and warm counsel greatly encouraged me.

Here was the first shipowner to clearly state that the Victoria's price was quite good. And the vessel could be brought to top shape again. There would be lots of work involved, and the Dutchman specifically outlined what to expect. But he also said, "Go for it!"

I had been praying, studying, and planning. In Switzerland we put together a complete feasibility study and went over it again and again. A good friend of mine, Joy Dawson, often states, "You must work like you never pray, and pray like you never work. Pray as though all depends on prayer, and work as though all depends on work."

At the suggestion of Iaian Muir, we renamed the Victoria ANASTASIS. In Greek this means resurrection.

Everyone involved remembers the day that Anastasis first moved: Not yet under her own power, tugs pulled her from her mooring to the Venice drydock. From there she would be towed to Greece for the refitting and overhauling of every motor and pump, and for the replacing of miles of electrical cable. Now the real work began.

The ship arrived in the Bay of Eleusis on July 5, 1979. Three years and three days later on July 7, 1982, we would sail.

"Because of the mercy ship Anastasis, Your Honor, I was in Greece."

CHAPTER
SEVEN

During the courtroom proceedings, I often thought of Deyon. I knew that she was praying for me. And I marveled at the fact that she was still alive. For as the dream of the ship had begun to come to life once again in Venice, my wife had nearly died in Lausanne.

It had all begun with the birth of John Paul.

John Paul was our only child born in America. He arrived ten days early but was a beautiful, blonde-haired, blue-eyed boy.

He had stopped breathing twice for a minute or two, and the doctor was a little concerned. Dr. Shenkle kept John Paul and Deyon an extra day in the hospital for observation. He explained that because we were going back to Europe, he needed to express some concerns.

Our little boy could have some brain damage. The fact that he had stopped breathing twice might be an indication of this. John Paul looked like a normal healthy baby. What could this possibly mean?

John Paul was now four weeks old and the time had come for us to head back for Europe. We boarded a British Airways flight at Dulles Airport bound for London.

Deyon had gone aft in the plane to lie down. She wasn't feeling well. Something was wrong. She needed to lie down again in the van on the hour's drive from the airport to Holmsted. We were planning to spend three days with family, but Deyon was increasingly in pain.

A local physician diagnosed a stomach ailment, gave her some medication, and recommended that we contact our doctor in Switzerland. So the next day we flew into Cointrin Aeroport in Geneva. Deyon went right to bed in the annex. Eliane Lack, a Swiss nurse and dear friend, telephoned Dr. Hajikani and he came immediately.

Deyon had a blood clot in her right lung. She began hallucinating as her temperature spiked throughout the night. Dr. Hajikani administered blood thinners and antibiotics and kept a close watch. But he really wasn't certain what the trouble was.

We had no medical insurance. Since Eliane was well-regarded in the medical community, our doctor suggested that Deyon's care be continued at home unless hospitalization was required.

This was a big week for us.

On Sunday we were to begin our first community service in the newly completed auditorium of the world-famous Swiss Hotel School, Ecole Hoteliere. A reformed pastor had come to me suggesting that we do something for the youth of Lausanne. The Ecole Hoteliere had agreed to cooperate, and our first meeting was to begin that Sunday evening.

We had prayed fervently for those meetings.

While driving to Switzerland to accept the responsibilities for the center, I had prayed for the entire region. In my mind's eye, I had seen little fires begin to glow all around the Lake of Geneva, and particularly in the Lausanne region.

I believed that God was saying that He had many people in this city. "Care for their spiritual welfare," He was telling me. This service was to be the start.

But Deyon got worse. In her delirium she would cry out for either Eliane or me. Her hallucinating continued. Sometimes she saw funny little creatures on the walls of our bedroom. At other times the apparitions were terrifying. She was gripped in fear.

Only as we gathered to pray for her, only as we specifically stood against the enemy, would her fears be quieted. None of this was at all typical of Deyon. She is a trooper. I was getting quite concerned.

Meanwhile, Sunday was coming closer.

What would I do with my wife so ill and the pressure of a new service? It was to be inter-denominational with many of the spiritual leaders from the regions participating. It could have a longlasting, positive impact on many lives. We could not cancel, but what should I do?

I believed and practiced that family was a greater priority than ministry. I taught that God must come first, family second, and ministry third. How was I to put it all together? It was to get worse before it got better.

On Sunday Deyon became gravely ill. We phoned Dr. Hajikani and he came to the annex and went right to Deyon. He began to move quickly and methodically.

"Eliane, telephone for an ambulance. Schedule an emergency surgery. Tonight. It seems as if Deyon has an abscess in the lower abdomen and it has been leaking. Widespread peritonitis has resulted. Her intestines have ceased to function. The pneumonia resulting from the blood clot and the general poor physical condition make her a poor candidate for emergency surgery. However, it is her only hope."

In two hours a meeting was to begin. I *had* to be there.

I knew that my place was with Deyon. I wanted desperately to get in the ambulance and go with her. I asked two friends to take Heidi, Luke, and the baby, John Paul. Then I knelt in prayer. It seemed that God was requiring me to go to the meeting—to begin the new ministry.

It was as though God showed me two things:

1. I could not add one day to the life of my wife. That was His responsibility.

2. He had commissioned me to do things that He did not personally handle. I was to lead His people.

I understood His message. I was to go across the street and lead the precious people there in worship and teaching. That was my God-given responsibility. He then would be free to do what only He could do—to take care of Deyon. Her life was in His hands, not mine.

It was one of the most difficult decisions of my life.

I walked into our bedroom, sat beside the bed, and took my wife's hand. She was so pale, so drawn. For ten days we had prayed earnestly for healing, restoration, and wholeness. God had been silent. And Deyon's illness had worsened.

Now the ambulance was to come. Once more we pleaded, "Lord, would You counsel us in this situation? Would You encourage us? Speak to us?"

A passage quickly came to Deyon's mind. I looked it up in the Book beside the bed. It was Genesis 23. The first words from that particular translation began: "And Sarah died being one hundred and twenty-seven years old. She was buried in Kiriath Arba, in Hebron."

That is not a very encouraging Scripture passage, particularly when received minutes before your wife is boarded into an ambulance for emergency surgery. Clearly her chances were not good.

Being the eternal optimist, I said, "Well, Sarah lived to be 127 years old, so it looks like you should have about 98 years left."

"Some encouragement," Deyon responded.

Then I explained that God was requiring me to go to the meeting. I could not go with her. How would Deyon take this? Would she feel that I was forsaking her in the hour of her trial?

No. She responded with great tenderness, "Don, if God is showing you to go over to the service, then you obey Him. He'll be with me."

With tears in our eyes, I bent to kiss her. I couldn't help thinking, "Will this be the last time?"

That five-minute walk to the auditorium was one of the longest walks I've ever taken. Never have I felt so alone. "Lord, how can You expect me to lead others in worship? I have never felt *less* like worshiping! I may lose my wife. There she goes in the ambulance. And yet You want me to worship— and worse yet, You want me to lead others in worship!"

Then it came, crystal-clear as the October air. *Worship is a choice, not a feeling. Choose to worship me for who I am. Others will then worship with you.* Worship is not a feeling, but a choice.

I remembered the first biblical usage of the word "worship," in Genesis 22. As Abraham saddled his donkey, gathered the firewood, and went to the mount, he requested his servant lads to remain behind. Then Abraham and his son went to *worship* the Lord.

Abraham's choice to worship required him to surrender his all to God, including his most precious treasure. Worship meant giving up his only son. And it was a choice.

I began to understand. God had something for me to do, and it would bless His people. But I must be willing to give all to Him. Only when all is given can He give back.

I entered the auditorium.

To my surprise, about 200 people were gathered. We had not advertised. *God must be about to do a wonderful thing here,* I thought.

I sat down next to my friend Tom Bloomer, who would lead the French-speaking ministry worldwide. "I want to slip out and go immediately to the hospital when we're through with worship," I whispered. Yet, as I was snapping shut the brass buttons on my leather Bible cover, I seemed to hear the Lord's still, small voice. *A leader remains* with his charge until all is finished. I unsnapped my Bible cover and began to worship Him. Then I knew His presence. That night was a powerful lesson in obedience.

Finally I rushed into the Hospital Cantonal de Lausanne close to midnight. Preparations for surgery had just been completed. They were rolling Deyon into the operating room. She didn't even recognize me.

Slowly, sadly, I drove home.

As early as possible the next morning, I went in to see Deyon. Tubes were coming from several parts of her body. She was hardly aware of my presence.

"What time is it?" she murmured.

"Eleven-thirty."

"Good, I've managed to make it another hour," she whispered. "It takes all my strength to make it an hour."

I stumbled out of the room.

Dr. Hajikani reported that severe complications made Deyon's condition and prognosis poor. Her lower abdomen had widespread infection. Her intestines hadn't functioned for several days.

Later she developed another blood clot in the lung. The day after surgery, her heart began to race. Its increasing rhythm and her falling blood pressure indicated that she might not come home.

I went to my little office above our annex. It was unbearably difficult to do, but I gave Deyon back to the Lord. She had been administered little pain medication due to the complications, and was suffering intensely. "If it's better for You to take her, I promise to trust You," I told the Lord. "I'll guard my heart against bitterness. Somehow, with Your grace, I'll try to go on."

I finally came to peace.

Within a couple of hours, I was to be right back on my knees. The struggle had returned. This process was to be repeated several times.

Daily, as I visited Deyon, I would read to her from the Book. Often the Psalms would be of comfort. On the third day following the surgery, I opened the Book to read as usual. This time I turned to Isaiah 34:16: "Seek from the book of the Lord, and read: Not one of these will be missing; none will lack its mate" (NASB).

It was October 20, 1976. God was promising me that I would have my mate. This was the first time God had told us that Deyon would live.

It took several weeks, but gradually she regained strength. Because of her need for rest and recuperation, we moved from the tiny annex to a large rented house by the forest.

This had been a time of intense, agonizing struggle. Yet on the horizon another great trial of a different nature would arise. And it would be confronted in Athens, not Lausanne.

CHAPTER
EIGHT

There had been many struggles in our years of mission work. And the crowded Athenian court-room seemed to climax them all. But as hours passed and the proceedings continued, my thoughts wandered to my faraway family, to another circumstance of testing, another trial, another time when God required my unquestioning dependence on Him.

It was February 1977. The baby was not doing well.

John Paul wasn't developing as the other two children had. He wasn't rolling over or sitting up. He didn't look at us. He seemed to always be staring off into the distance.

All during Deyon's illness she had been unable to care for John Paul as she so wanted. She was fighting for life and strength. Even to hold him during those first few weeks had almost been more than she could bear.

Now we telephoned for an appointment with the

pediatrician. "Bring him in next Tuesday," we were told. Like typical anxious parents our concern bordered on real worry. What was wrong with our blond-headed, blue-eyed second son? He was so unlike his brother Luke, who had smiled and laughed as a baby. Both Heidi and Luke had walked early. Were our expectations too high? Or was something really wrong?

The pediatrician examined our five-month-old boy. He seemed to think that we were overly reactive. John Paul was just slower than the other two. "Throw away the growth and development books," Dr. Frank kindly advised us. "They'll only induce you to make comparisons between the children."

But we still suspected that something was wrong.

At nine months we were certain. He still didn't roll over or sit up. He still had that faraway look in his eyes.

We contacted another pediatrician recommended to us by Dr. Frank. That physician suggested yet another doctor, a specialist who took care of children with special needs.

What did this mean, "special needs"? What was wrong with our boy?

At 14 months we admitted John Paul to the University of Lausanne hospital for eight days of intensive testing. A visiting Australian specialist in different forms of retarded and brain damaged children was taking a sabbatical for further research. He agreed to see John Paul.

He had virtually every test available. The results confirmed severe brain damage which had occurred early in pregnancy. The cause was unknown.

What would this mean? For us? For little John Paul?

He was named after John, my maternal grandfather from Norway, and for my father, Paul. We had such plans for his life. Any father imagines the avenues that his progeny will someday travel. I so wanted this son to have my grandfather's heart for God.

I had long heard the stories of how the man had loved God's Book and people. His warm, compassionate heart and eyes, described to me by my mother, made me want to know him. Unfortunately, he had died before I had had that chance.

I wanted this son to have the diligence and character of my own father. I wanted the things I so admired in the last two generations to be passed on. That is why we had named him John Paul, using both names together.

His blue eyes and light blond hair gave him a striking physical appearance. His brain damage gave him unusual movements and severe retardation. It was hard.

My greatest hopes for this little one now seemed totally unattainable. Even basic skills such as feeding himself, sitting, standing, and personal hygiene would require years and thousands of hours of effort to develop. Everything that comes so easily and naturally for normal children would cost John Paul greatly.

Why me? I wondered in my heart. *Why us?* Hadn't God called us into a public service ministry? We couldn't retreat or hide. What would all of this mean for the rest of the family?

Deyon and I had similar experiences. Hers came

first and was really the genesis of my later struggles.

During John Paul's eight-day hospitalization, she drove 20 minutes to the hospital to visit him. She would quickly finish the breakfast dishes, take Heidi to school in Villars-tiercelin, and drop Luke at the Wright family with his friends. Then she would rush on to arrive at the hospital as early as possible.

Her heart full of a mother's expectancy, she would open the door to his hospital room, searching for just one small sign that her son knew his mother—a glimmer of the eye, a curving of the lips into a small smile. Even a movement of the head would show that John Paul was aware she had just walked into the room. But there was nothing. He didn't even realize she was there.

I was away in Australia at the time, teaching in a conference and discussing the ship.

Deyon had to face this Gethsemane without me —all alone. She poured out her heart to the Lord. Driving home from the hospital, she let the tears flow. But they couldn't wash away the hurting pain. There was no glimmer of recognition, no response from her little boy. Her heart was breaking.

For eight days in a row she drove to the hospital and ascended in the elevator to his room. For eight days in a row she got into the car and drove home. Her son never knew she had been there.

She had given birth to him. She had bathed him every day. She had fed him almost every meal he had ever eaten. She had dressed him in his clothes. She had changed his diapers. She had combed his hair.

In a sense, his very life depended on her.

Yet John Paul didn't even know who his mother was.

Every parent of a handicapped child asks the question, "Why me?" The real question is better put, "Why *not* me?" There is no plausible explanation for why not me or why not us.

We believers are not better, not wiser, not more worthy of special shields to protect us from the hurts and pains of this world. Our difference as followers of Jesus is that we have a God who understands suffering and injustice. He was innocent, yet suffered unjustly that we might not suffer eternally.

Deyon began to question God in her heart, but not in a cynical or bitter way. Questions of thirst are rewarded with the water of understanding. No water is sweeter.

God, do You understand? I need a relationship with my child. I feed him. I love him. I clothe him. I care for him. I bathe him. I carry his life close to my breast. I put my arms around his precious little body. He never responds. God, do You understand?

Slowly, ever so slowly, light dawned within her. God was questioning her. Did she not understand how God had felt for thousands of years? His heart was broken far beyond her comprehension. He understood the mother's heart. He had created mothers.

The Father feeds. The Father loves. The Father clothes. The Father cares. The Father longs to have a relationship with His sons and daughters.

But here is the difference: John Paul *cannot* have the relationship; he is handicapped. Mankind *will* not; he turns the other way. God the Father calls to all His sons and daughters. He calls to every heart.

Deyon related how God had often spoken to her about the areas that handicapped her spiritual growth. Sin damages us all: Our growth is stunted, our vision blurred, our understanding hindered. All because of sin.

Yet God still loves us. He still pursues us. He still calls to us to come to Him.

As we now look back over the 8½ years of his life, John Paul has been used by God to teach us much. We all love him dearly. Each little piece of progress has been a major milestone for our whole family. We celebrate his gradual development with joy and praise.

As he has learned, we have learned too! One of the first things that any parent must develop is *acceptance*.

Each gift given by God is unique. Each child is special, and not to be compared to others. And each handicapped child's parent must accept two things.

First, this little handicapped child is "ours." Some parents struggle and never accept the child as their own.

Second, it doesn't really matter how or why this happened, or who is to blame. That kind of thinking will not make the situation go away. Instead, it makes matters worse, especially when we blame ourselves. Condemnation will eat away at self-respect and leave the parents sociologically handicapped.

We also learned the importance of *humility*.

It is difficult to be in public with a handicapped child. An awkward gait or ill-timed noise is not always easily handled. It is humbling to have a child who never quite fits in with all the rest. It is humbling to identify with the weaker, abnormal elements of society.

This should not be hard for Christians, but it is. Christ calls us to help the poor, the helpless, the needy, yet we often struggle with this call.

General William Booth, the founder of the Salvation Army was derisively called, "General," by news media and publicans. However, his consistent, humble identification with the social problems, the hungry, and the homeless, eventually brought him to an audience with King Edward. When the Monarch of the British Empire called him General, it became a title of honor.

John Paul is teaching us humility.

He has also increased our level of *patience*.

We've had to continually readjust our expectations because of his limited performance levels. Everything comes slowly, by degrees, for John Paul.

It took him seven years to take his first faltering steps. He still has not learned to crawl. Fine motor coordination is severely restricted. But when he took those first seven or eight unassisted steps, the house came down! We burst into applause. What an achievement!

I believe that God responds in a similar way when those whose lives are deeply scarred by sin begin to walk the pilgrim walk. It should also bring the whole Christian family to their feet in respect and appreciation.

Our other three children—Heidi, Luke, and Charles—daily identify with a weaker member of the family. He has taught us to be tolerant of others.

One of the greatest lessons learned through John Paul, our special little gift of grace, had to do with me personally. I have always felt very uncomfortable around handicapped people. I've never known what to say. My awkwardness always seemed to make the situation worse.

I was unable to handle suffering. I found avoidance was the best way for me to deal with those in distress, but this was often seen as rejection. John Paul has helped to change all that for me. Compassion is a by-product of suffering.

Things could have been much worse. He could have been violent or self-damaging. He has always been a peaceful child. At times, however, discipline has been required to keep him that way. We've discovered that biblical principles of child-rearing apply to our brain-damaged son just as thoroughly as to our other children.

The first time he received a spanking (according to Proverbs 13:24), we did some soul-searching and discussing first. We certainly didn't want to damage him any further.

His refusal to go to sleep at night was an enormous pressure on the entire family. Getting him quiet took hours. He would fuss and fuss, cry and carry on, and then eventually out of total exhaustion drop off to sleep. Then he would be in terrible shape the next day. This cycle grew increasingly difficult. It had to be broken or it would break the family.

Again Deyon suffered the most. John Paul called out to her again and again. A drink of water, a back rub, a caress. What would it take to get him to sleep?

We really weren't sure how to handle this special little boy. We didn't know if we should, or could, change his negative behavior patterns, but we needed to lessen the wear and tear on the family. And, even more important, help this little one develop as peaceful an existence as possible. But after looking into the Bible, talking with others, and reading much material about autistic and brain-damaged children, we realized that pain was a deterrent to undesirable behavior. We were rewarding his negative behavior with positive reinforcements. Instead, he must be disciplined. He needed help to break the cycle.

He cried hard, shocked at the mild spanking I administered as lovingly and firmly as I could. It was very lightly applied, but it was a new experience for him. Such actions from someone with whom he was most secure clearly indicated that his behavior was not acceptable!

It worked. He changed. I am convinced that this is partially why he is so content today. He is secure, able to recognize negative behavior. Like other children, he wants to be sure of what is allowed him.

Simply leaving him in a room to cry all by himself, didn't produce any changes. He required loving, wise discipline. To discipline is to love, but it is never easy. There are many ways and means to discipline. Each child is unique and great sensitivity is required to train and guide him to maturiy. Yet, child rearing is simple enough that any parent, if he follows biblical principles, can adequately and properly fulfill his obligations.

John Paul probably responds best to me, his father. He has often felt the pain of my disapproval when his misbehavior had to be redirected. But he also laughs loudly when I rough house with him. And he smiles at my noisy, silly games.

Some people wonder why we haven't sought miraculous healing for our son. I do believe it is possible. I've listed all the miracles of the New Testament and believe that the only case of God restoring damaged brain cells was in raising Lazarus from the ead. His brain-wave response must have been completely flat. Dead cells. Clinically dead. Yet when Jesus called Lazarus to come forth, his brain cells were totally made alive again. So it is possible.

We believe that God is capable. Never would we want to even suggest that such a healing was beyond the capacity of God. Perhaps it is timing. Perhaps God is not yet finished with using John Paul in our lives. Perhaps it will be a long time before such a healing takes place. Meanwhile, we have come to accept John Paul as he is. Healed or not, he is a privilege, not a curse.

In all of us, *character* is what God stresses— integrity and character. These are more valuable than gold. And each is unattainable at any price unless consistent choices and moral principles have produced them over the long haul.

Heidi, Luke, John Paul, and Charles love for Dad to tell stories. They like the humor of the early escapades of my life and the stories about God's provision.

I developed an acrostic with the word *character* to assist me in coaching my family toward the Lord.

"C"—CONFIDENCE IN GOD. Psalm 78:5-7.

It is my responsibility as their father to show them by example that God is completely trustworthy. If they trust me, they will probably never struggle with trusting God. (In later years pastors, teachers, and other authority figures will bear the same responsibility.)

So I tell stories. The three jostle for position to sit on Dad's lap or to snuggle as close as possible. John Paul usually wins the seat on the right knee, even though he really hasn't had to struggle.

"Do you remember about the castle in Germany? It's a gold brown color with a turret and a courtyard. There are several rooms for children of all ages to play in. It is not too large, but we did house several hundred there during the 1972 Olympic Games outreach.

"We had no money and only a dream. God helped us buy that castle when we didn't have anything. The reason God wanted such a center for us was because of His love for people. He knew that we would use this Bavarian castle to tell others about Him."

As I relate story after story, the children develop confidence in God. I try to show them what each remaining letter of the word *character* means.

"H"—HEAR GOD SPEAK. John 10:3.

"Every living human has a conscience. It's one of the great distinctives between man and animals. That conscience helps us to please our God.

"Sin dulls the conscience. And it keeps us

from hearing what God has to say."

Each of my four children will one day have to make major decisions on his own. Each must learn to hear from God individually. Heidi and Luke already have consistent, daily times of reading in their own Bibles. This is probably the most important way of hearing from God. But His "still, small voice" spoken into the conscience of our minds is also valid. Great tasks require great guidance. Mary was to give birth to the Messiah and an angel came and clearly communicated to her God's plan. To say that God cannot speak just as clearly today, severely limits the unlimited power of God.

I recommend Loren Cunningham's book *Is that Really You, God?* I believe it is a classic on divine guidance. It can be easily read by inquiring young minds.

"A"—ACCEPTANCE OF SELF. Matthew 19:19.

Self acceptance gives us a sense of belonging. It gives us a sense of direction and confidence.

A good self-image can be developed in every child. I explain to my foursome, "Love builds and encourages. Hatred destroys and damages."

I want my children to love the unlovely and the lonely. Actions speak so much louder than words.

Compliments build confidence. Rewards for achievement and excellence of any sort bolster confidence. But praise must have quality to it, and not be just empty flattery. Flattery deceives. Praise propels to new goals.

"R"—RESPECT FOR AUTHORITY. Hebrews 5:8.

Each man, woman, boy, and girl has to deal with many authorities every single day of his life. Even simple transportation could not occur without the authority of the yellow line and stop signs. The relativity of truth destroys the foundations of society and personal interaction. Absolutes are absolutes.

Authority can and even must be questioned. But underneath must lie the bedrock of appreciation and respect for law.

"A"—ATTITUDE. 2 Timothy 2:2,15,24.

A negative attitude can destroy the greatest of opportunities. Negativism and defeatist attitudes are largely a result of choices. Deyon's father used to correct her by saying, "Get happy!" which was, of course, the last thing any child wants to do. Happiness has to do with choices. We can get glad the same way we got mad—by choice. Problems arise every day, but they need not determine a defeatist destiny for anyone. Consistent choices to view life positively will produce contentment.

A positive attitude does not imply naivete. It is rather the absence of a negative bent in our minds. A good, hard look at the facts is always a prerequisite for wisdom. But negativism dwells on weaknesses rather than on strengths.

In telling stories to my children, I have retold the pure, Western wisdom of my father's colloquial words, "Can't never did anything," and, "You'll never know until you try."

"C"—CHOICES.

Deyon and I have always allowed our children many choices. However, not all choices are options for their level of responsibility. Luke still is not given his choice about certain food items. Although he wants the choice of what goes on his plate, that decision happens to be his mother's. She prepares the proper menu for nutrition and a balanced diet.

Character consists of habits and customs. Consistently good choices produce consistently good character. Habits make up our way of life. Choice is the razor's edge between moral integrity or moral morass.

"T"—TRAINING.

My high school coach had such a positive impact on my young, formative years. He was a good example for the development of manhood. Coach McKinny took us through all the stages of training. He continually stressed the basics. Character was important to him. Leadership was developed into our impressionable minds as a very desirable and attainable goal. He took us through the steps of a master trainer.

First, he did it for us.

Second, he demonstrated how it was to be done properly. He always took the time to show improper execution, so we could learn the difference.

Third, he explained thoroughly how we were to do it. His goal was for each of us to learn to do it as well as he did.

Fourth, he allowed us to do it, mistakes and all. Quietly he encouraged our success. Silently he disapproved of our mistakes. He knew that he would sit on the sidelines in the real game, and at that point we would have to do it ourselves.

Finally, he coached from the bench. He was not "on the field" with us, but on the sidelines, coaching.

This will forever be a reminder for me as a father. I must go through all these steps. Yet by the time my children are teenagers, I must stand on the sidelines of their lives and coach. My role will simply be to advise and counsel, not to live their lives for them.

"E"—EXCELLENCE.

Our competition should not be against our fellow participants in the Christian life. Instead, we should test ourselves against our own personal standard: What are we really capable of doing? We must strive for excellence. Reach for the best. Practice. Train. Work. Pray. Believe. Obey. All these actions are energized by the work of the Holy Spirit in the believer's life.

Yet God is a forgiving God. When failures come, He restores our relationship. Then, once again, He encourages us to strive for maturity, for our very best.

Our children have been taught that their *best* is all that is required—not the highest score in the class and not the fastest time in a race. Someone will always be brighter and faster, but each child should make his best effort. That brings satisfaction and fulfillment. It points competition back toward their own performance. In America, where sports reign supreme, we believe that it is important to focus these children on their inward performance, and not in winning over someone else.

Yes, we want them to win, but not at the cost of character.

"R"—REPENTANCE.

To accept the blame when failure or sin has occurred is also paramount to character. Only when we humble ourselves before God and man will weaknesses in character be cleansed. Repentance is necessary to build solid, good character.

Heidi and Luke each have their favorite tales of times when Dad had to say he was wrong. I needed to ask their forgiveness. This restores respect and trust in any relationship.

Trust seems to have two parts.

First, trust is based upon performance. Low performance equals low trust. Good performance allows for great trust.

However, trust must also have grace—grace to allow someone to fail and then to trust him once more. Trust is given and taken away mainly through performance, but we must always be willing to trust again. God does so with us.

We hope we have taught all of our children as much as they have taught us. But little John Paul has been particularly used to show us the tender, compassionate heart of God.

Just recently he said, "Ma, Ma, Ma," when in a difficult position. He was clearly calling for his mother to help him. We both rushed into the room to find him almost ready to fall to the floor. His call might have been undistinguishable to others, but to us, his mother and father, it was a clear, trumpet call from our son. He needed our help. We responded with total commitment.

How much like our God!

He responds to our muffled, garbled communication. To Him, our Creator, our needs are perfectly understandable. We cry out. He responds.

And as our deeply troubled world cries out, we Christians must go to the rescue. We must be the hands and feet of our God. We must embody the

One who always helps the helpless. A cry for help. A response. That is why the Anastasis was in Greece.

That is why I was on trial.

CHAPTER NINE

The trial had forced me to take a second look at the events surrounding our efforts to launch the mercy ship. And I was reminded of the supernatural ways in which God had confirmed the work of our hands.

The Anastasis lay in the historic Bay of Eleusis with her seven-ton anchor at six cables. This protected harbor had seen the world's first naval battle. Xerxes and the Persians were defeated in a nautical conflict that was probably the greatest single influence in fifth-century B.C. Greek history.

Our mercy ship was also destined for battle. Her weapons would be nonnuclear but far more powerful. Every birth is a battle. We had been commissioned in the eternal battle to give spiritual birth to a powerful ministry tool—a ship to serve the nations. War would be waged—not war *against* people, but a war to *save* people. It was a war to do good, a war to help the helpless. It was a war with prisoners, but at the end was victory.

Our weapons would seem cumbersome and ponderous to many but familiar to everyone who has followed God. Praise, prayer, the Bible, faith, fasting, witnessing, holiness, and perseverance would bring down the strongholds of the enemy in Jesus' name.

Our strength would not be in megabudgets but in *people*—people who hungered to know God and make Him known. Our greatest gift would be people—people whose level of commitment more than compensated for the small capital base of our pioneering work.

From 25 different nations God's people would leave houses, land, family, and friends to join together to make a dream become a reality. Doctors, engineers, navigators, welders, evangelists, mothers, college students, pastors, nurses, and teachers (some with their children) would link, hand-in-hand, to win this battle.

Before us stood the impossible. Beside us stood the Lord.

Like David and his sling, we could either focus on the giant or on God. David took five stones. I've often wondered why. Perhaps he wanted the security of an extra four in case he missed. Perhaps he was thinking of Goliath's four brothers and wanted to be prepared.

At times in my life I have found myself focusing on the Goliaths in front of me. However, I am learning to realistically establish the cost, then go for the victory.

As I climbed the companionway from our cabin on the upper deck to the conference room on Lido deck, my mind was wondering what would happen in our meeting today.

Captain Ben Applegate would be sitting beside me. His being there would give me strength. He and Helen were not only Captain and Mrs. Applegate; they were tested, true friends. They had survived the loss of the first ship.

Captain Ben's father had been the mayor of Great Yarmouth in England. The proper thing for a young man like Ben was to choose either the military or the merchant marine officers' school. Ben chose the officers' school. He was bright and graduated one year ahead of his class and a few months later, he was an officer cadet on the bridge, sailing out of South Hampton for New Zealand.

God graced Captain Ben and Helen with six lovely children. Sue, the eldest, had worked with YWAM in Amsterdam. There she met and married Mounir, a young Egyptian medical student. Mounir returned to Alexandria with his bride to complete his medical studies.

One morning I received a phone call from Austria. The somewhat shaky voice on the other end of the line explained a tragic death. I didn't know what to do. How was this possible? Quickly, I took a notebook and pen and hurriedly wrote the details as I knew that many questions would be asked of me.

After a long prayer for grace and wisdom, I placed a person-to-person call to New Zealand to Captian Ben. Somehow , as tenderly as possible, I gave them the message. Sue was dead. She had been buried in a cemetary in Alexandria ten days before. Telecommunication had been impossible.

Only days later had someone been traveling out of Alexandria to Austria.

I knew that Sue was not the first child the Applegates had lost. A younger child, Jenny, became ill as a five month old baby. Her sickness had not been properly diagnosed and she was left blind, deaf, and crippled from meningitis.

Captain Ben and Helen were not committed Christians then. They had taken Jenny anywhere they thought they could receive help. And yet her condition only worsened. Eventually, a Pastor wisely and lovingly counseled them.

Through their sorrow and struggle, when Jenny died at the age of five, they found life in Christ. They were able to forgive those who had missed the diagnosis. In the valley of suffering, the anvil of anguish had forged a compassion and character in both of them. Their hearts would be forever sensitive to the sufferings and struggles of others.

Today we faced other obstacles. Together we had to confront immense difficulties. We had a ship. We had a dream. We had people. But we also had Goliath-sized problems. Our auxiliary boiler had just been condemned. Would the ship ever sail? What could we do? Those were the questions that flooded the minds of the men who gathered together there with me.

One of Lloyd's surveyors had suggested, "Sell the ship." Our chief engineer, John Brignall, had thought, "Impossible. This is God's ship and He will have an answer." I marveled at his faith. I could only see the giant.

How much would it cost? Would we ever find a replacement boiler? The marine architectural work to design a new one to our specifications would take six months to a year.

All had to be approved by Lloyd's and then the boiler would have to be built. That would take an additional six to nine months. Each weld would have to be inspected by a Lloyd's surveyor. Everything would have to conform to the highest standards of the shipping industry.

We would have to pay a great deal of money for such a major replacement of essential equipment. And we didn't have a penny toward it.

Giants can loom quite large in our minds. But now was the time to take our eyes away from the giant and focus on God.

The other men at the table seemed to feel much like I did. There was David Cowie, a New Zealander from Lake Tekapo; Jack Hill, an engineer and excellent Bible teacher from Canada; the captain and staff captain, Ben Applegate and Hal Burton; Alan Williams, the fiery evangelist and ship's chaplain. All seemed to be staring straight into the giant's eyes. And so was I.

In spite of our sense of foreboding, we knew that all was not lost. We would go to God in prayer. He had faithfully led us to this point. He would have to provide an answer. Somehow, somewhere, God had a solution. We prayed. We tried to look at God, not the impossibility of the hour.

Suddenly the phone rang. The chief engineer answered. We could tell that he was speaking to the Lloyd's surveyor. Could an answer have come almost before we prayed?

He hung up, smiling quietly, and explained. A Greek shipowner had ordered a new boiler over a year ago, then had sold his ship. The boiler met our specifications and was just one mile down the road, ready and waiting for us! It was already surveyed. It would fit. It would even save us money.

We wouldn't have to sell the ship! God be praised, He was greater than the giant! And how much would it cost? Tens of thousands or even more?

We began the negotiations with the company. They needed to sell and we needed to buy. Each party was happy and a reasonable price of just over 22,000 dollars was agreed upon. Our Goliath was down!

Unfortunately, he wasn't the only giant. He had brothers. And some of them seemed even bigger. Like the giant of human need, for instance.

I have often contemplated the overwhelming needs of humanity: the starving babies of Ethiopia, the huddled masses along the Cambodian borders, the 35 million people that will inhabit Mexico City in the near future, the Calcuttas and New York Cities of our needy world cities, that sometimes suffocate our small attempts to help.

Someday we will stand before God. He will not be satisfied with the fact that we knew how great the need was. He wants us to be assured that He is even greater, that together with Him we can make a difference.

The psalmist wrote, "As for the days of our life, they contain seventy years, or if due to strength, eighty years...for soon it is gone and we fly away" (Psalm 90:10 NASB).

The majority of citizens of Western nations born after 1950 will live to see the year 2020. Most of us can look forward to a lifespan of 74 years. However, for the citizens of Ethiopia or Chad, 40 years is all that can be expected. Today we have 4½ billion neighbors plagued with disease and a lack of food and water. Half of them are unreached with the life-changing message of Christ. In 2020 we will have 8 billion neighbors and many more Goliath-sized problems.

Jesus commanded us to go and minister in the middle of this need. He is the only true Source of life and hope.

When the 5000 people were hungry and requiring food, the problem must have seemed like a Goliath to the disciples. They knew that only one boy had his lunch. Yet as they obeyed Him and broke the bread, multiplication took place. The giant of human need was met and conquered through their participation.

Before the good news about the boiler arrived, Captain Ben had looked around the table at the rest of us. And he had confessed doubt. This came as a shock to some of us. Our captain? Doubting?

His doubt involved the number of qualified technical crew that we would need to properly operate such a large ship. We desired to strive for excellence. We wanted the ship to be a credit to the name of God. Without enough properly trained men, this goal could not be reached.

I could understand Captain Ben's dilemma. And I had an area of uncertainty of my own. I looked around the table. "Do any of the rest of you have any doubts?"

The remaining giants suddenly appeared as we began to honestly open our hearts to one another.

One giant was the required finances. That was my Goliath. Another was the amount of alterations and repairs needed to be able to use the ship as we believed God had directed.

It was soon evident to all of us that in our minds, the greatest battlefield of all in spiritual warfare, we were crippling God with our unbelief. Doubt paralyzes. It doesn't really affect God, but it certainly colors our receptivity and attitudes. Doubt prevents our receiving all He wants to give us.

We began to confess to Him and to each other our sin of doubting. Then we realized that we were probably not alone. The rest of the crew members were quite likely struggling with the same thoughts.

Our entire crew gathered in the International Lounge, the largest public room on board the ship. It was originally a bar and ballroom, but would soon become a sanctuary where God could meet us through the preaching of men and women, and through the study of His Word.

Following the example in Zechariah 4, when Zechariah and Zerubbabel faced the mountain of impossibilities in rebuilding the temple and wall of Jerusalem, we took immediate action. The completion of that work was promised by the man of God. And the hands that had begun the work completed it with shouts of "Grace, grace!" (Zechariah 4:7 KJV).

If this church could do such an unorthodox thing in a service, then surely we didn't want to be so proud as to resist any action that would help us break the steel bands of doubt that plagued our minds.

All of us began to shout, "GRACE, GRACE!" to the impossible Goliath-sized giants that had intimidated us.

GRACE, GRACE! to the mountain of human need.

GRACE, GRACE! to the lack of workers.

GRACE, GRACE! to the repairs that must be completed.

GRACE, GRACE! to the finances that must be given.

GRACE, GRACE! to the people of Greece.

The meeting was not over. We went on. Many different crew members wanted their particular part of the vision to be included in this time of release. To these added requests, we all shouted, "GRACE, GRACE"! However, shouting "grace, grace" does not in itself repair a ship. And God was not merely repairing a ship. He was the same wise God who worked with my dad through the sorrel stallion colt. God was using a ship to train an army. A spiritual army.

We would face many giants with our mercy ships and their ministries. Such confrontations are a normal part of Christianity, and especially in missions. If we expect to be effective, there are bound to be adversaries.

It was a unique "slingshot" that God used to shake the hearts of people in the Greek countryside. There was no mushroom cloud of an atomic explosion, but there would be a mushroom of media exposure. The weapon that God wanted us to use was not a newly designed, technological breakthrough. It has been around for some time, never improved upon. It is the weapon of prayer. Prayer and fasting.

I was invited to speak at a ministers' conference in Germany. Dr. Wolfhart Margies, Baptist pastor in West Berlin, shared the teaching with me. As Dr. Margies began one of his messages, I knew that God had a message for me and the ship. He asked a simple question: "How do you start a ministry?"

The different responses from the audience were all good and correct. Someone suggested, "With a clean heart." Yes, the need for purity is a prerequisite for power in a ministry. Another suggested, "With praise." Judah, which means praise in Hebrew, went before the soldiers. Yes, this was also important. Still another suggested that "much time in the Word" was necessary, and "in serving others," or "being discipled by another." Each was necessary and good, but was not how to begin.

Dr. Margies asked us to remember how Jesus began His public ministry. Like an arrow of truth, the message pierced my heart. Jesus was the Messiah. He was the Son of God. Yet He had begun His public ministry only after 40 days of *fasting and prayer.*

In a world so geared for planning, goal-setting, and human strategy, this message was pregnant with meaning. Every man there remembered how he had or had not begun his public ministry. Many could remember years of study in seminary or theological training. Others could remember associate pastorates or small churches before moving to other locations. How many could remember a serious period of fasting and prayer?

The truth of Dr. Margies' teaching grew in my

thoughts as I boarded a flight back to Athens. Forty days. Fasting. Praying. How should we arrange it? What would be the best? We had women and children. Others worked 16 to 18 hours a day. Teams were out ministering. I met with the other leaders and bared my heart.

We were rapidly approaching the end of the work necessary to take our sea trials. We were nearly ready to sail to the needy of the world. What would our public ministry be like? Powerful or powerless? Potent or impotent? Loving or harsh? Compassionate or callous?

We all agreed: We would fast as a community. It would be voluntary. We would divide the 40 days into segments, with each of the five leaders taking one segment. The crew and community could join as they believed appropriate.

Virtually everyone joined in the fast. Some took a day or days a week, others took longer periods. Even some of our children fasted meals or a day.

We were denying the natural desire for food and spending that time alone or in groups in intercession. We would follow Job 42. Job prayed for his friends. Our prayers would focus on others, not on ourselves.

We interceded for the lost. We warred against the evil forces holding so many millions in moral darkness. We prayed for exposure of organized crime. We pleaded for justice and peace.

Above all, we focused much concerted prayer on the land of Greece. We asked for blessings. We prayed for the Word of God to be read and understood in this land of early Christianity. We prayed for new apostles like Paul and Silas to be raised up from among the Greek youths that came to the ship or our temporary living quarters. We prayed for the many businessmen with whom we had daily contact. We prayed for the government and the future of the nation.

Then it began to happen.

God began to do something that we will long remember. It was almost unbelievable, yet 175 people from more than 20 nations witnessed it. Cameras recorded the event. Even a home movie documented it.

A crewman named Moustafa, a North African believer raised in Islam, was walking down the beach in the area of Kinetta. This is about halfway from Eleusis to Corinth. Our crew and their families were renting the seaside bungalow at Kinetta Beach from the owners.

Moustafa made a peculiar discovery as he moved along the water's edge. Twelve fish left the water and swam ashore. Now fish don't normally "swim ashore." This phenomenon had Moustafa's complete attention. He had actually watched them flop out of the sea and into the rocky, tidal area.

He quickly picked them up and headed back to show his friends. As he had learned while a boy in North Africa, he prepared them over an open fire for a few of his friends who were not fasting on that day.

I didn't give this too much attention. I actually didn't quite know how to handle the situation. I wanted to believe Moustafa, but I grew up fishing for trout in the rugged mountains of Colorado with lures and hooks. I had spent entire afternoons without even seeing a fish. And I had certainly never seen a fish jumping ashore. I was cautious. Besides, the fish weren't very large—only eight to ten inches long.

The next day the Brignall family were seated for their evening meal. John, the chief engineer, was off the ship and with his family. No one is more practical and logical than our chief engineer. Seated at the Brignall table were their two sons, David and Richard. The family looked in amazement as 15 to 20 feet away from their table at the shoreline a large fish jumped ashore!

Richard quickly rushed from the table and grasped the fish before it could maneuver itself back into the sea. This was a perfectly healthy live fish, somewhat larger than those that had jumped ashore the previous day. Most fishermen will attest that fish don't normally jump ashore. Richard prepared it, and several ate some of it or at least had the pleasure of tasting a bite.

Now I thought I could explain, at least to myself, the reason for the earlier 12 fish jumping ashore: Perhaps this fish was chasing down a meal.

Then on Sunday morning at 8 o'clock, the thirty-sixth day of the fast, it happened again.

Becky Howard, from Dallas, Texas, was reading her Bible and having her daily devotional just in front of the bungalows. She glanced up to see fish starting to come ashore. They literally jumped out of the sea onto dry land!

Becky quickly began to gather them up. Several Greek families were also there and joined her effort. Becky brought 210 fresh fish into the galley to be cleaned. There was a fresh fish for everyone who was not fasting. And we have no idea how

many the Greek families gathered up—they took
their fish away with them.

I began to understand that this was not going to
be easily explained away.

Then two days later, on the thirty-eighth day of
the fast, Tuesday, November 24, 1981, at eight in
the morning, just as we were gathering together in
groups for intercession, it began to happen again.

My wife, Deyon, ran to where I was praying with
the other leaders. She called, "The fish are jumping
out of the sea again!" None of us could stay in the
prayer meeting. We had to see this for ourselves
with our own eyes, and touch with our own hands.

Just in front of where we were living in the
rented facilities, fish by the tens and fifties and
even hundreds were jumping ashore. We gathered
fish for a long time. We used two wheelbarrows
that belonged to the bungalows to help cart fish
back to the galley.

I am not a skeptic, but I am a realist. I bent over
and caught one or two of the fish just as they were
jumping ashore. I flipped them back into the sea
but they swam straight back toward the shore and
jumped out again!

The clear waters of the Aegean Sea allowed us
to see 15 to 20 feet into the water. We could see
no large fish feeding or chasing the others. There
was no pollution, as in the inner harbor, close to
the city. There was no reason that any of us could
find for the fish to jump ashore.

We cleaned fish for hours, until nearly ten that
night. There were almost two tons of fish! We put
them in groups of fifties, then hundreds, for ease
of counting.

We counted 8301 fish before we placed them in large barrels of plastic, quickly purchased to preserve them in.

It was like a modern parable. We serve a God who can miraculously provide. He was encouraging our efforts in the harvesting of the nations for righteousness. There would be a mighty harvest on the earth, and the mercy ship and many others would be a part of that great harvest.

We gave special attention not to miss any fish. Some Christians in evangelism are not concerned about the safekeeping of the harvest, but it must be kept by all means. We gathered all we could find. Later we found only 12 fish that had been missed. They were caught in the crevasses of the rocky surface.

Our Norwegian chief cook, Trond Olson, was aptly prepared in preparation and preservation of the fish. They became known as the "miracle fish," and we delighted to tell others about what had happened.

Almost immediately, our evangelism efforts were more effective. It was as though God had given an affirming miracle as a sign to the people surrounding us. This event was reported in the newspapers and was even mentioned on Greek national television.

To my knowledge, this is not a regular occurrence in Greece. Perhaps there is some perfectly logical explanation as to why this happened. There could also be a natural explanation to the Red Sea drying up before Moses and the children of Israel, but that does not stop me from believing that it happened. I believe both were miracles. God has always been at work in human history. His purposes are profoundly furthered through such acts. The very first miracle that Jesus did was the turning of water into wine. The only possible reason for this miracle is that Jesus did not want a family to suffer embarrassment. There does not have to be a great motive or need for God to work a miracle. He loves us and knows what we need.

The fish jumping out of the sea certainly encouraged each of us. We saw it happen right before our eyes. We saw other impossible things happen also. The giants were being removed from the landscape.

The gospel was being preached and people were responding. The finances were coming in. The ship was being repaired. Our sailing date was approaching. The crew was being trained—qualified professional people. Our prayers were being answered.

Little did we realize that one of the Greek people so positively affected during this very time would have a relative who would again tower on the horizon as yet another impossible giant.

The mother of young Konstantine seemed to increase her animosity toward us at every sign of progress we made. The more her son read God's Word, the more anger she directed our way.

Shortly, she would take some kind of metallic object and break some of the windows at Costas Macris' Hellenic Mission Union.

It wasn't a metallic object that Mrs. Douka chose to use against us. Nevertheless, the news that Alan, Costas, and I would stand trial for a criminal offense was similar in its impact upon our mission and our ministry. It was unexpected. It was shocking.

It was shattering.

CHAPTER
TEN

The trial was taking longer than we had expected. And we felt a certain sense of futility, for it was becoming apparent that the judges might have some preconceived notions. As the testimonies dragged on, I thought of this land of Greece—the time we had spent here, the friends, the fasting and prayer, the miraculous fishes. And I clearly and joyfully recalled the day we finally set sail from our sheltering Greek harbor toward our mission field—the world.

The starboard windlass ground counterclockwise as the anchor slowly came out of the water. The chief mate, Denys Collins, himself a master mariner, noticed that the anchor was fouled.

We were "stern to," sandwiched between nine or ten other ships in the Mediterranean mooring style so often employed by the Greeks. It was almost like seeing a row of ships "parked" alongside each other, and made fast with both anchors down.

The ship next to us had her anchor across ours. Seven tons of anchor plus four cables of anchor chain made for a very difficult situation! The small channel off the Island of Salamis and the Chandris shipyard was not wide enough for us to turn the 522-foot vessel.

The third mate, Menno Gort, used the experience he had gained in maneuvering the small coastal vessels he had once captained. Along with the bosun and able-bodied seamen, he freed the cable.

The forward tug was signaled by the pilot and ever so slowly we made our way out of what we had come to think of as a ships' graveyard and into the open sea. Here was the moment for which we had all worked, prayed, fasted, believed, sacrificed, and hoped. Tears welled up in my eyes.

The fouled, twisted anchor cable was like the graveclothes that bound and twisted around Lazarus. When Jesus stood before the tomb as he was about to raise His friend he said, "I am the resurrection and the life."

Life had come into a dream that had been dead—God's dream and our dream. The ship ministry that had become a "cross" to the mission and to so many of us was now moving under her own power.

Every engineer had worked for this moment. Every mission member had prayed and believed for this hour. People around the world had believed in us and with us. Our faith had not been in vain.

The great white mercy ship cast off the lines of the tugs. Captain Ben said goodbye to the pilot as he descended the ladder on the ship's side onto the waiting launch.

The captain gave his first orders as master of the Anastasis. "Steady as she goes," he said. The helmsman responded, "Steady, sir." "Engines full ahead." The mate responded to the captain's orders by repeating the command and signaling the engine room on the telegraph. "Both engines full ahead, sir."

Everyone who was not on watch was on deck looking at the familiar Greek coastline fade into the distance. Piraeus, the port so easily recognized by thousands who have sailed over the centuries, shrank away on the port side. The Acropolis, perched high above the city of Athens, reigned proudly over myriads of apartment buildings that seemed to diminish in size as we moved along.

We were on our way to Malta, the island nation that gave us our first registry. There we acquired the Maltese Cross shipping flag that we would hoist in city after city. The points of the Maltese Cross stand for the nine Beatitudes of Matthew 5.

Ever since the apostle Paul arrived in Malta after a 14-day storm at sea (as recorded in Acts 27 and 28), this island nation has stood as a bastion for historic Christianity.

Some of the earliest mercy ministry was done through the Knights of St. John of Malta. They established hospitals along the major trade routes in the Mediterranean, and were known as the "hospitalers." They followed the example of the Good Samaritan in providing for both physical and spiritual comfort. Here we found the two hands of the gospel once again: The *proclamation* in one hand and the *provision* in the other.

As the Anastasis sailed across the Mediterranean, we were pleasantly surprised at how well she handled. She was surely a ship for the sea. God be praised!

On the horizon, visible in the early-morning sea mist, was the huge fortified city of Valetta, Malta. We spent three days there in the nation of our registry. We met with many believers and were greatly encouraged. They had been praying for us for several years. Some of those men and women were close friends.

The cobblestone streets and quaint little shops were a welcome sight to all the crew. The ship was again Mediterranean-moored, with both anchors down in the Grand Canal and the mooring lines aft to the quay along the roadside. She was at that time Malta's largest vessel. Her gleaming white hull had been given two coats of a special polypropylene paint.

This mercy ship has a peculiar power to pull from deep within the heart of those who view her a tidal wave of praise to God. This has often amazed me. The Maltese reacted just this way. The sight of the mercy ship, gleaming white in the harbor, caused spontaneous praise to well from their lips. "God be praised! He is faithful!"

Resurrection had indeed occurred. God's ship, a salvation ship, was in their harbor. It seemed to give hope, to inspire and fuel their prayers. The lies whispered by the enemy in silence were exposed through glorious reality. The white hull seemed to say "holiness" and "purity."

Later, in other port cities, men, women, and

children would remark that something happened the moment they came aboard. They were aware of the presence, the peace, and the joy of God.

This is what we had fasted and prayed for. This was the beginning of the answer to all our prayers. God was speaking to people by His Holy Spirit. The love of the crew toward each other was very evident, as well as their love for God and their love for people far different from themselves.

The mercy ship is really a miniature Christian United Nations. Many races, many languages, and many cultures share one common goal: to know God and make Him known. They long to serve the nations in Jesus' name, to meet the needs of the hurting, the hungry, the homeless, and the hopeless.

As the mercy ship sailed past the breakwater out of Malta and on past the outer marker toward the Panama Canal, my heart was again full of praise to the Lord. I was not aboard. Instead, I stood high on the parapet of the old fortress, above the Grand Harbor in Valetta, watching the ship sail into the distance. After their 21-day voyage I would see my wife and three sons again. Heidi, my daughter, stood by my side. We waved and watched together.

David Boganrief, raised in the Salvation Army, had his trumpet on the aft deck and played a beautiful farewell to Malta. The crystal-clear notes of the accomplished trumpeter echoed across the sandstone buildings.

The heroes of World War II had fought for this island and her people. Now there were committed believers in Christ battling again for the redemption and future of Malta. Their weapons were familiar to us on the ship: prayer, faith, and obedience to the Word of God.

Heidi also had tears in her heart as we watched the ship sail round the corner and out of sight. It had been a busy schedule. Much effort had gone into getting the ministry developed. However, my greatest responsibility was not to the mercy ship but to my own family. Father and daughter needed time together.

The early Moravians under the leadership of Baron Nicholas Ludwig von Zinzendorf had established the fact that the nuclear family was the most basic unit of the church. Each man was to be prophet, priest, and king for his "natural congregation." I could not abdicate my responsibilities for relationship with my daughter and delegate her instruction to others. Others would greatly help and instruct in areas beyond my training, but she and her brothers were primarily my responsibility.

Actually, this was not the first time we had traveled together. We had flown to England when she was five or six. We had traveled by car to Germany for several days while her mother, Deyon, was taking care of our two-day-old son, Luke. She had also accompanied me to Scotland. There we attended a teaching conference by day and witnessed in the Edinburgh streets at night.

With the joy of a proud father, I was watching Heidi grow into a young lady. Her consistent, daily time in the Word gave me peace about her commitment to Christ. Our entire family had a mission. It took both hands and most of our efforts, but it was a joy.

Heidi's French was much better than mine. When we wanted a private conversation, we would often revert to the language of her early education.

On this occasion she was to fly with me just before her twelfth birthday, when ticketing was still 50 percent of the adult fare. After this, cost would prohibit indiscriminate travel. Now it was good for the two of us to be together.

Deyon and I tried to practice the principle that family came before ministry and that God was above all. It is not always easy to keep this balance. However, at times like this, compensations such as transcontinental flights seemed to more than make up to Heidi for her sacrifice of sharing Dad with so many other people.

I knew that it was quality time my children really needed. It wasn't the amount of time I was with them that counted, but my undivided attention and generosity of spirit. Often fathers are tempted to be generous only with money. But it is generosity in giving of oneself in scheduled quality time that the child so desires. It makes a statement that will stand the test of time. It writes indelibly on the heart, "My dad cares. He puts me above other pressures. He is willing to sacrifice other things to have me with him."

So Heidi was strapped in the seat beside me. Our Alitalia plane took off from Leonardo Da Vinci airport outside Rome and winged us toward our native America. Somewhere down below us was a white ship bearing our precious loved ones.

The Anastasis' arrival day in Los Angeles was historic. More than 3000 people stood on the shore at Pier 53 to welcome the ship into the City of the

Angels. Breathlessly we watched her come alongside and make fast.

Our friend Melody Green was there. It was one of her first public appearances after the homegoing of her husband, Keith. Just as the mercy ship and her crew came into view, large speakers filled the air with Keith's recording of "Holy, Holy Is the Lord."

I looked around. Everywhere believers were praising God with tears in their eyes—tears of joy, tears of celebration, tears of recognition of the God we serve.

Loren and Darlene Cunningham, Jim and Joy Dawson, Rich Buhler, John Dawson, and representatives from other missions and churches were at the microphones. Landa Cope was rushing everywhere, making certain that the day was an honor to the Lord and to all those who had helped make this day possible. Landa had been a close family friend for ten years. Now she had the responsibility for the San Pedro Port office.

Somehow the day brought healing. Many in the audience had dreams that had crumbled and died, just like our first ship. To see what God had done brought resurrection hope and understanding to so many. Some people who were far from God came simply to satisfy their curiosity and were moved by the Holy Spirit.

While the ship was approaching the wharf, a small twin-engine Cessna 310 circled above. Piloting the plane was the father of a family that had found Christ and reconciliation in recent months. The man's daughter had told him of the mercy ship. He had scoffed in response.

"Someone's big idea. It will never work. Too expensive. Too big. Too much work. Too many technical people required to operate it." Those familiar five giants attack everybody!

As the Cessna slowly turned above the great white ship, Keith, the father piloting the aircraft, whispered to God, "Wrong again, Lord. Please forgive me."

Keith and Cynthia and their children soon became friends of ours and of the ministry. Their warm, open personalities and exciting charisma captivated many of the Anastasis crew. With them, something was always happening that was of interest to all. Keith walked the decks in the engine room and above the bilges. He questioned everyone he met. His inquisitive mind was searching to find how God had enabled us to accomplish our task.

Little did we realize how significant was this friendship. This family would make a noteworthy investment into the kingdom of God. The hand of the Lord was already upon them. Soon He would use them even more.

The Christians of southern California responded to the needs of Guatemala. The biblical Christian president, Efrian Rios Montt, had issued an invitation through Oren Paris, our mission director for Guatemala, and through Loren Cunningham. President Rios Montt had requested assistance for the affected hill tribe people, the Ixil Indians, whose crops and villages had been ravaged by the guerrilla warfare.

The dock in front of the ship was covered with cargo. This cargo was not for commerce. It was to be distributed in Jesus' name. Almost a million dollars' worth of goods were waiting to be given away. This was almost the same amount of money the ship had originally cost!

I thought of the ways of God. For years we had sacrificed to develop a ministry that would cost one million dollars just to get started. Then God allowed our first major port-of-call to present gifts of love in Jesus' name, of close to the same value!

A Los Angeles company donated food so that the hungry might eat. Tons of corn meal, culturally acceptable to the Indians and commonly used as their staple food, were among the first pallets to be hoisted on the cargo slings.

The local stevedoring union was wonderfully cooperative. They came and loaded the ship free of charge. Everyone seemed to want to be a part of a ship that would bring goodwill to hurting people. This act of generosity was to be repeated by stevedoring and wharf unions almost everywhere the mercy ship called.

One of the managers of the World Port in Los Angeles remarked that previously he had not believed in miracles. But when the stevedoring union volunteered to load the cargo for two solid days, free of all charges, he considered that a miracle in the category of the crossing of the Red Sea. Los Angeles stevedores, thank you! Much of the world has heard of your act of mercy and kindness.

Once again the anchors were weighed, and Captain Ben called for both engines "Full ahead." The work in Guatemala was soon accomplished. After Champerico, Guatemala, our course would cross the equator and the international dateline. We were headed for the northern tip of the North Island in New Zealand.

The sixth of February, Waitangi Day, is celebrated as New Zealand's national day. The earliest ships had arrived at the Bay of Islands at Opua. Now the Anastasis would be part of the 1983 ceremonies in this jewel of the Southern Hemisphere.

There in New Zealand an early-morning telephone call started my day with excitement. Keith, the California businessman from the Cessna 310, was on the other phone, calling halfway around the world from Jacksonville, Florida.

I could hear the seriousness in his voice. His foundation had purchased a small ship. It had been a passenger/cargo combination used in the Maritime Provinces in Canada. The small ship was 173 feet long and had a draft of 11½ feet. Originally she had carried 102 people as well as 12,680 feet of cargo capacity. Dry cargo and refrigerated cargo could both be carried.

His family had flow in to join him on the ship. Maine lobster had been the meal of that evening just before Christmas. The family had looked forward to using the ship as a yacht for pleasure, as well as for gospel ministry.

But now Keith felt the Lord speaking to him. If they used the ship several times a year the first year, how many times would they enjoy it the second and third years?

I knew how much he longed to stand at the helm and pilot his own vessel. Keith was a real entrepreneur. Yet he was allowing God to mold and build his life. He was a good, trusted friend. What

was Keith leading up to? What was the purpose
of his satellite phone call?

He explained that it was late at night in Jacksonville. He was actually outside the ship on the wharf
speaking into the phone. I could picture the situation easily in my mind.

Keith described the small vessel—her excellent
condition and her potential as a mercy ship.
Maintenance work had already been completed on
her in the Bellinger Shipyard at Jacksonville. She
wore a new coat of white paint. Her former public
rooms could be used for training and teaching and
discipling of the followers of Jesus.

Keith's description had changed. He was no
longer talking about a yacht. He was describing
a mission ship. This was the real story in his heart.

"Cynthia and I have discussed and prayed about
the ship, Don. We have talked it over with the
family. We want to give it to you."

I didn't quite know what to say. We had worked
so hard, prayed so much, believed so long for the
Anastasis. We had taken second mortgages on our
mission property to be able to buy the Anastasis.
God had required that we be willing to risk
everything. Now here was a man wanting to give
us a 500,000-dollar ship!

There were no strings attached. It was truly a
gift: no debts and no major repairs. It was just out
of dry dock and newly painted. Everything was
functioning well and there was fuel in the tanks.
It was truly a sacrifice to God from a family that
had found Him.

Keith was still speaking on the phone. "I know
you will use the two hands of provision and

proclamation to preach the gospel. The hungry will be fed. The hurting will find healing. The lost will be rescued. The lonely will find their Friend. The story of the Good Samaritan will come to life through the work of this little ship."

Keith wanted to know right then—that very instant. "Don, will you accept this gift? I need to know, now. I know how all you YWAMers always pray about everything, but I need to know. Now!"

I bowed my head and said, "Yes, we accept the gift to be used in God's work." Then I felt immediately convicted.

What if this were a distraction? Was it really God at work? Could it weaken our efforts and divide us? How could I have said that we would accept it so lightly? *God forgive me!*

I quickly left my cabin. I ran across the passageway to find Alan Williams. Alan would be able to pray with me. He was a vital part of the leadership. It was not really my prerogative to commit us to anything totally without submitting the matter to those who worked closely with me.

Before the ship had departed from San Pedro, California, another member of Keith's family had wanted to give Deyon and me a beautiful four-wheel-drive Chevrolet Blazer. As we prayed seriously about the matter, we believed it would not be right to accept the gift. Kevin had passed his test in giving his prized possession to the Lord. We had passed the test of giving up unnecessary material possessions in saying, "No, but thank you."

But this wasn't a four-wheel-drive. It was a half-million-dollar ship.

Alan and I bent our knees and bowed our heads

before the Lord. We didn't want anything to take root in our hearts that would distract or weaken the purposes of God for our lives. After some time together in prayer, we were both certain that this too was of the Lord. We couldn't have guessed that eventually Alan and his wife, Fay, would multiply the ministry in themselves. They would become directors on board that very ship!

While in New Zealand, the news of Hurricane Oscar also reached our ears. Fiji and Tonga were partially devastated. Buildings were blown down, schools demolished, churches leveled.

Operation Good Samaritan was born: *provision and proclamation.* The islands had suffered, and it was Christian compassion that would minister the love of God.

It was quite an effort to gather relief supplies for the hurricane-affected South Pacific. New Zealanders from all walks of life, Rotary Clubs, businessmen, Lions Clubs, Jaycees, and various churches worked tirelessly to meet the needs of their Pacific neighbors.

Two New Zealand men, Mike Raymond and Bryan Archer, caught the vision and ran with it. The Governor General, Sir David Beattie, was contacted. He agreed to lend his name as the patron of Operation Good Samaritan.

The cargo holds were offered free. Churches and missions as well as some civic clubs were challenged to "fill up the ship" in order to help the victims of the hurricane.

Sawmills donated building lumber. Companies gave roofing tin. The City of Auckland Fire Department gave five fire engines in very good condition as gifts to the Fiji Fire Department. Sewing machines were loaded for a girls' school. TEAR FUND (The Evangelical Alliance Relief Fund) would place many cubic meters of prefabricated, hurricane-resistant houses in the cargo holds. And again, the stevedores loaded the ship at no charge.

With 337 people on board, the Anastasis sailed from Auckland harbor after a farewell attended by many friends and supporters, including the soon-to-be-elected Prime Minister, David Lange.

We had gone all the way around New Zealand, visiting 15 cities of the two islands. We had been in the country for a total of five months, spending two to three weeks in most cities. Many lasting friendships were established during this first visit of ours to the land.

We thought we would be ministering to the islands of the Pacific, but the islanders were the ones ministering to us! As the cargo of love was offloaded, the Fijians and Tongans seemed to embody their own history.

Only 150 years before, on sailing ships, the life-changing message of Christ had first entered these islands. Tall-masted ships had arrived with John Williams, John Smith, and many others. They began to learn the language and customs of the people.

Fiji would end the cannibalism and warfare that so weakened her families. Instead, she became a leader in the proclamation of the gospel of peace. Young Fijian men and their wives preceded white missionaries to the highlands of New Guinea to plant themselves, even to give their lives for this new way of life. They willingly offered themselves as a sacrifice so that others might hear the good news.

For four generations, King Tuafa'ahau Tupou IV and his royal forebears had served the God of Christianity. Tonga had converted almost en masse to this superior religion. The King's great grand-father, King Tupou, was a change agent. He was aware of the power of the spirit world, and he sensed in the early missionaries a greater power.

That first mission ship had anchored just off Nu'kualofa. The message was already halting the wars in Fiji. Could it be possible that the message was so powerful that it could change men's hearts from evil to trust?

Now, in 1983, the great-grandson of King Tupou, and his brother, the prime minister, welcomed another mission ship into their harbor.

This time lumber was being freely given to rebuild their nation. Many churches opened their doors to the teams from the mission ship. Some-thing had been broken in the spiritual realm. We could sense it. There was a new freedom. Old bondages and new deceptions were somehow be-ing exposed for what they really were.

God was moving in the hearts of these people. They wanted to join us, and join us they did, from Samoa, from Fiji, from Tonga, and from New Zealand. Many people boarded the ship to join her on her missions of mercy.

As we sailed from Suva, Fiji, hardly a dry eye was found on deck. Several hundred Fijians and Fijian Indians gathered to say farewell to the mercy ship that had brought so much love and help.

On board, one of Fiji's outstanding young men,

Rusi, the son of Dr. and Mrs. Mataika, was sailing to unknown destinations. Like Abraham, he was leaving his home to bring blessing to the nations of the world.

Hundreds on shore sang an old Fijian hymn. The melody floated across the water and seemed to fill the ship. Then Dr. Mataika led everyone in a prayer for his son and the sons of Fiji about to be used in the work of God.

I could not help but think of my father and thousands of other fathers who had given their firstborn and their lastborn to the Lord, because He had need of them. There could be no greater gift. No greater sacrifice. No greater reward. No greater privilege.

Rusi prayed from the rail on the upper deck. He asked God to bless his native land, to honor her for giving her sons and daughters for the greatest and highest of all causes, the cause of Christ. "Bless Fiji," he prayed, "with an outpouring of revivallike fire, through the preaching of the gospel and through the reading of God's Word."

Father and son, each saying goodbye, neither knowing when or if they would ever see each other again. Sorrowful, yet rejoicing. Father watching the lights of the mercy ship as she sailed through the coral channel and off into the night. Son on the decks watching the fading lights of his homeland. Eternity ahead of them. History behind them. Thousands and thousands of others marching beside them to bring the good news of the Prince of Peace.

After the work in Fiji and Tonga was completed, the Anastasis reloaded in New Zealand. A shipment of lumber donated there would help build the Pacific and Asia Christian University on the big island of Hawaii. By that time the mercy ship had ministered for 18 months to more than 400,000 people. Thirty-four different cities had felt the impact of her mission teams, freely offering the grace of God with two hands.

The medical ministry was still developing toward its full potential.

The dental clinic on board was complete. Dentists had even taken the two portable dental units to minister on a remote island in the Pacific. Our doctors had also gone ashore and given health care to every inhabitant of that small Fijian community.

An X-ray unit had been installed and was available for any emergency.

Yet the dream that God had placed in my heart was not yet fulfilled. I discussed it with the three doctors on board. Much study and planning had already gone into this. Consultation with other leading medical professionals had brought us to the same conclusions.

Life-changing surgery for eye diseases, as well as plastic surgery for clubfoot and cleft palate maladies, should be carried out on the ship. We all knew too well that a clubfoot in the developing world could quite possibly relegate a child to the life of a beggar, or worse. Cleft palates also left their victims weighed down with severe personal difficulties.

And we would develop an eye room. Eye disease and infections plague the Third World.

Surgeons could volunteer their time and expenses for scheduled three- and four-week missions of mercy. Our medical staff could take care of the postoperative recuperation and the scheduling of the actual surgeries.

One of the doctors, Dr. Christine Aroney, would be responsible for the advance planning and liaison with local hospitals.

Another of the doctors was more concerned for preventive medicine in primitive or otherwise needy areas. Much of the world's health problems can be directly traced to impure water and lack of hygiene.

Dr. Peter Lucas had already served as a medical missionary in Nepal and was well-qualified to develop this aspect of the mercy ship medical ministry. Dr. Peter hoped to see mobile medical teams able to depart the ship in four-wheel-drive vehicles or on a mobile launch. This would give access to those remote areas that are so often overlooked or inaccessible because of inadequate transportation.

There was much to do! The ship was en route to Hawaii for a short stay. She would then move on to the Pacific Northwest, where many of these plans would be fully developed.

On the horizon our eyes began to focus on the highest point of Mauna Loa. Our Hawaiian destination was finally visible. To some degree I could identify with the early missionaries as they arrived after more than 164 days of sailing into what has been called "Paradise." Fortunately, our voyage from New Zealand had taken us only two weeks.

It was now 6:30 and we were only 20 miles out. Our coworkers in West Hawaii would soon be in their 7:15 A.M. prayer meeting. Had they yet noticed a great, white ship in the distance? They had prayed and believed with us that one day the ship would anchor in Kona Bay. In the distance it looked like someone was waving a sheet. Yes, with the binoculars, we thought we could see people. We weren't due until tomorrow, but they had apparently sighted us anyway.

Soon island dugout canoes came around the bend to pick up Captain Ben, the other officers, myself, and our wives. I thought of the early brig, the Thaddeus, that had dropped anchor in this very bay. On October 23, 1819, it had arrived. With the same timeless message of Christianity they had sailed from Boston. We had sailed from Auckland, New Zealand.

Along with city officials and about a thousand well-wishers, Loren and Darlene waited there on the sandy shore. That day will be forever etched in our memories as a fulfillment of God's promise. Loren, who had originally had the dream of a mercy ship, had released his vision to me. Now together we shared in its fulfillment. It was the resurrection for many who had prayed and believed.

For me, it would also bring about my trial by trial.

The mercy ship had 337 people on board representing 25 different nations. We offloaded the lumber at the port of Kawaihae. Then we weighed anchor and sailed to Hilo. This historic city had seen a great revival in the 1800's. Twenty thousand Hawaiians became a part of church fellowships in just four years in the early 1840's. We had many friends in Hilo, and after fellowshiping there, the ship sailed to Maui.

The United States Coast Guard boarded the vessel. Everything seemed to be in order. The check was a routine inspection of a vessel registered in a foreign nation.

Much research and advance work had gone into bringing the vessel to the U.S.A. Every shipping company knows only too well the number of regulations and pecularities involved in entering American waters.

We had a letter from the Chief Legal Counsel for the Treasury Department, responsible for the movement of ships. They stated that our wives and children were not passengers, for they had paid no fare. The British have carried wives and children for years under a classification of "supernumeraries."

No nation had ever yet questioned the British practices.

But the Coast Guard took exception. American shipping has only two categories, "crew" and "passenger." So they disagreed with the classification of the vessel. According to their interpretation, the women, children, and students in training were all passengers. Even though another Department of the United States Government had given a different legal ruling, everyone would have to disembark.

The Coast Guard is a part of the Department of Transportation. They all read the same rule book. But they came to different conclusions. And our own conclusion was clear:

You can't fight city hall!

So we began a long process of changing the classification of the ship and her registry. And we began to make some major alterations.

Just over three miles of pipe would be installed

for a sprinkler system. Work would be started on an auditorium for 600 people. A classroom would be developed in a portion of the cargo area. This would allow closed-circuit televising of surgical operations, teaching from hospitals, and other areas of service.

A local company offered a bid of 3 million dollars for the work. Instead, we began to do it ourselves with volunteer help. It cost us only a fraction of the bid.

The 700 Club gave us television coverage of the situation and volunteers came from all over the world to help the mercy ship. They came from the United States, Canada, Europe, Scandinavia, and the Pacific. With their assistance we were able to complete the work ourselves at a fraction of the cost.

To stand before the 300 people on board and explain that the ship was stopped was one of the most difficult things I have ever done. It would have been even worse if I had known it would take over a year to restore the vessel to full ministry capability.

I couldn't believe that the ship was being stopped after so many hours of prayer and work to get it started. Yet when God allows something to stop, it stops.

I thought of the apostle Paul.

In Acts 16:6 Paul was stopped from going in the direction he had planned. He said the Holy Spirit hindered him. We read later in Galatians that he was ill when he first preached the gospel to the people of Galatia.

Perhaps it was this very illness that the Holy

Spirit used to stop the apostle Paul. If so, I suppose God could just as easily use the United States Coast Guard to stop us.

> Consider it pure joy, my brothers, whenever you face trials of many kinds, because you know that the testing of your faith develops perseverance. Perseverance must finish its work so that you may be mature and complete, not lacking anything (James 1:2-4 NIV).

A miracle would have been nice right then. But miracles are signs; they do not produce character. We had seen enough signs along the way. Now we needed perseverance. Besides, God had something else in mind.

In compliance with a joint resolution of the U.S. Congress, President Reagan declared 1983 as the Year of the Bible. Before 3000 leaders from across the nation at the annual National Prayer Breakfast, the President of the United States made the following declaration:

> Today our beloved America, and indeed the world, is facing a decade of enormous challenge. As a people we may well be tested as we have seldom, if ever, been tested before. We will need resources of spirit even more than resources of technology, education and armaments. There could be no more fitting moment than now to reflect with gratitude, humility, and urgency upon the wisdom revealed

to us in the writing that Abraham Lincoln called "The best gift God has ever given to man. . . but for it [the Bible] we could not know right from wrong."

The Honorable Herb Sagawa, Majority Leader of the Hawaii State House of Representatives, was named the Honorary Chairman of the Hawaii Year of the Bible Committee. Loren Cunningham became the State Director.

Churches and groups from all over the island rallied to put a New Testament in every home in Hawaii. New Testaments were printed in Chinese, English, French, Hawaiian, Ilocano, Italian, Japanese, Korean, Laotian, Portuguese, Samoan, Spanish, Tagalog, Thai, and Vietnamese for distribution in the Asian Pacific melting pot of Hawaii.

The Anastasis crew, students, families, and volunteers would take part in the distribution along with many churches. The plan was well-organized. Everyone was ready when the day of Bible distribution arrived. If people were not at home, their book was placed in a rainproof plastic bag and left hanging by the door. Hardly anyone refused the special Silver Jubilee and Statehood edition of the New Testament.

After the Bibles were all distributed, the captain and I received a plaque honoring the participation of the mercy ship crew. This award was given for our efforts in distributing hundreds of thousands of Bibles to hundreds of thousands of people.

How strange! The following year I would be in court in another country. And I would be on trial there for giving away one Bible—to one boy.

CHAPTER
ELEVEN

I had only 15 more days of freedom. Despite the fact that Alan Williams and I had received no official notification (we heard by word of mouth!), we would soon find ourselves on trial in a foreign country. Our mercy ship was docked indefinitely in Honolulu. It was December 6, 1984.

I walked out on the foredeck. I passed the hatch covers for the cargo holds, the windlass, and the anchor blocks. In the forward eye of the ship was the outline of a cross. It had been fabricated in our on-board metal shop by one of the men. He had made it in gratitude to God for the changes in his life.

I studied the cross. Was a cross being placed before me? Was it the will of the Father that I should suffer through imprisonment? Would I have to be away from my family? What would I do in prison? I knew the passage in 1 Peter 4:19:

So then, those who suffer according to
God's will should commit themselves to
their faithful Creator and continue to do
good (NIV).

I tried to push these thoughts into the depths of
my subconsciousness. Yet they kept floating to the
surface just when I didn't want them.

I turned around to face the bridge of the
Anastasis. Flying from the yardarm was the
American flag.

That flag, so symbolic of freedom of conscience
and freedom of religion to most of the world, was
waving in the cool Pacific breeze. In my country
all faiths were free. That only became possible
through Christian tolerance and charity. The
deeply religious separatists who sailed from
England in the seventeenth century had greatly influenced the forming of our constitution.

In the England that flourished before Wilberforce, Whitefield, and the Wesley brothers, a Baptist or Separatist could find himself in prison
simply for not belonging to the Church of England.

Our early forefathers resisted state-enforced
Christianity. True Christianity was a condition of
heart. It changed governments. It did not need
government protection. The very protection
seemed to indicate a weakened, adulterated condition.

The founders of the American Constitution were
not prejudiced in religious opinion. They held a
high view of human dignity. Men and women had
a basic right to worship God as they chose. To leg-
islate any type of worship placed the government

in a position of usurping God's rightful role.

Freedom of speech is an absolute necessity for the propagation of religion. And to restrict the propagation of religion is to enslave the conscience of man through government intervention. In America, the open exchange of ideas was provided through constitutional guarantee and due process of law.

The battle I was facing had been fought before— many times before. To have those Stars and Stripes flying as the ensign from the halyard, many people had to be willing to make the supreme sacrifice. To fight for freedom was an honor. It would never be an embarrassment.

Deyon stepped out of our cabin onto starboard upper deck. That 175-square-foot room had been home for more than five years. We loved the compact but nicely decorated quarters. Everyone on board a ship knows what it is to live in small spaces. Our wide-open commission to minister to the world's needy more than compensated for the cramped conditions.

She called softly to me. It was almost time for the evening meeting in the International Lounge. She knew that I liked to be alone with my thoughts before any public gathering. And she had understood why I had left the cabin to go forward to the fo'c'sle.

With Alan and Fay Williams, we climbed the stairs into the beautiful forward lounge of the ship. We had named this the "International Lounge" because representatives of so many different nationalities had heard the life-changing purposes of God there.

The room had recently been restored to its original condition. With the installation of the sprinkler system as recommended by the U.S. Coast Guard, all the deckheads of the ship had been taken down. Miles of welded pipe had been installed. The deckhead in the International Lounge was silver leaf sprayed with a gold lacquer. Those who had worked on it were volunteers. The quality was outstanding. They did it to honor the Lord.

The room was full. Some sat on the floor. Alan and I were about to say goodbye to these dear, trusted coworkers of ours. In less than two hours we would begin our journey to the Athens trial.

After each of us spoke briefly, the Executive Council of the Anastasis gathered around and prayed for us. That was our best possible farewell.

We descended the stairway and returned to our cabin. This time all the family was gathered in the one room. I looked at each of the four children.

Heidi, almost 15 and the eldest, seemed to be handling the situation well. Luke, 11, was quiet and thoughtful. He wasn't quite certain how to express his heart's uncertainties. Charles and John Paul seemed unaware of the possible consequences to their father's impending journey.

Deyon and I gathered them all around and committed each other to the will of the Lord. We asked for God's grace to be upon us all. Each would need that particular gift, and our God has promised that more than sufficient grace is available for every situation.

We had already discussed the situation thoroughly. The children knew that I was going to a trial. We had listed the possible outcomes from such a situation. We had talked of my not going back. Greece was such a long way from the ship. Wouldn't it be easier simply to never go to Greece again?

I had listed each of those possibilities.

The only honorable thing to do was to return to Greece—to stand with Costas Macris, to represent the rest of the victims of former dictatorial laws. I would go, even though I had done nothing wrong.

If I hadn't gone back, I don't think I could have respected myself. To return for the trial would illustrate the New Testament's teaching of love for the brethren.

After saying goodbye to each of the children, Deyon and I crossed the passageway to my office. I wanted some time alone with the one who had given me four lovely children. It wasn't so much what we said to each other, for we spoke only a few words. It was just being together. The thought of not being together for months or years made the moments costly indeed.

Deyon is a great source of strength to me. She had no small part in the founding of the ministry of the Anastasis. She takes regular prayer walks with the Lord. She has done this for years as a way to exercise, to get outside, and most of all to have an uninterrupted time of prayer.

On one of these many prayer walks, she believed that God had indicated that prison was more than just a remote possibility. We had discussed this openly, with the ramifications for our family, our ministry, our relationship, and our friends.

Now we were saying goodbye, facing an uncertain

future. Was our confidence in a secure future or in knowing God who *is* the future? We chose to put our confidence in Him.

Deyon is always practical-minded. She had visited the women's section of the Koridallos prison in Athens. The wives of our leadership team had taken care packages and Bibles to the female inmates. She knew far better than I what I was facing.

She had packed my suitcase for the cold, merciless Athens winter. The greatest request from women inmates in the unheated institution had been for gloves and socks. Damp cold penetrated deeply through the stark interior of the prison walls.

Only once had I been stopped by the police for preaching on the Greek streets. Alan had been taken to the police several times in and around Athens. Once a chief of police actually told him to continue on. "Preaching is good! It counters the influence of sexual immorality and drugs!" Alan was informed. Neither of us was ever arrested or booked in any way.

Nevertheless, Deyon had packed my suitcase for jail. Warm socks. Old clothes. I had to change a few of the items in order to be presentable in the court.

Just as I was to leave Deyon in my office, I realized that I had no reading material in my briefcase for the long journey. On my bookshelf was a thin, gray paperback that I had purchased a few years before. I had never read the book and had actually forgotten the subject matter. I was looking for something light to help me pass the time.

The title of that thin gray paperback was *These Fifteen,* subtitled "Pioneers of the Moravian Church," by Edwin A. Sawyer. Those 96 pages would hammer truths and history into my heart while in the aircraft.

I boarded the 11:30 P.M. American Airlines flight from Honolulu, knowing that I had only one day to spend in Los Angeles at the mercy ship's Port Haven in San Pedro. There an old hotel had been renovated for ministry and communications. It provided a home port for the ministry of the two ships, Anastasis and Good Samaritan.

I was struggling so much with the uncertainty surrounding the trial that I had postponed the very important task of writing the Anastasis' newsletter. What could I write about? I was hesitant to discuss the trial. There were too many unknowns, too many what ifs. And I didn't want to alarm people.

As the staff in the Port Haven at 709 South Centre Street in San Pedro gathered around, we began to discuss the newsletter together. The word "insecurity" kept coming to my mind.

I knew I shouldn't be insecure. I had a loving family. The crew and staff of the two mercy ships were loyal and committed to follow Christ. The ministry was effective. Everything pointed toward security, not insecurity.

If only I didn't have this Greek trial hanging over my head! The trial and one or two other situations were stirring up a turmoil in me. Why was I so disturbed, so uncertain and concerned? "Be anxious for nothing, but in everything give thanks to God." Yet I was still struggling.

Openness. That was what God was requiring of me. He wanted me to be open with the others so that we might learn together. None of us had ever faced a "trial for our faith" in a courtroom before. Insecurity was to be expected. If it wasn't there, then I had failed to realize the possible implica-tions of the trial.

The words of my high school coach came back to me. Drill. Know the basics. Practice. Be pre-pared. How very important it was to have a pre-game talk! I needed to discuss every option with those who work with me. Put it all out on the table. My dad seemed to be saying again, "Speak your mind, Son. Get it out in the open so we can deal with it and others can know what you are facing."

I needed to resist the pride that sometimes keeps me closed up, the desire to stoically go it all alone. Those temptations are common to many of us. We were designed to need both God and our fellow-man. The one who truly goes it alone is truly alone.

We sat in a corner room overlooking the Los Angeles harbor, with its ships coming and going up and down the channel. Together we began to list the possible cause of our uncertain emo-tions. Those precious staff members were also feeling insecure, as well as the ship's crew. We faced so many unknowns. And the possible ulti-mate consequences of the trial troubled each one of us.

I read from the life of Paul in Galatians chap-ter 2. Even that great apostle, the flagship of the early missionary movement, had been in-secure. That was at least somewhat comfort-ing. He had returned all the way to Jerusalem

because of insecurity about his ministry.
The list before us began to grow.

Fear of Man:

Was I too concerned about what others would
think about the director of the mercy ships being
on trial? Yes, I was. I wondered about those who
don't know Christ. How would they relate to a
man who had been condemned as a criminal? The
antidote to fear of man was to trust God more. He
was in control and has all wisdom. I knew His
character. He is totally trustworthy.

Fear of Rejection:

I had so labored with others beside me for the
mercy ministries of the ship and for the mission.
How would my coworkers react to the charges
against me? Would I lose meaningful relationships?
Would others not want to associate with me? I
thought of Jesus—rejected by all. He was willing
to suffer rejection for my salvation. I repented.

Fear of Failure:

Fear of failure can paralyze us into total inaction.
I was extremely grateful for the mission of YWAM.
The others on the International Council, and
especially Loren, had loved and trusted me enough
to risk failure. And the cutting edge of possible
failure sometimes keeps us on our knees, therefore
assuring success through grace.

Some of our most dramatic growth springs out

of failure. Hadn't the mission learned its greatest lessons after the loss of the first ship? God measures failure by different standards than ours.

Fear of Success:

Success puts unbelievable demands upon people. Was I afraid of the demands upon my time, my family, the mission, the ships? Was I finding comfort in the insecurity and lesser demands? Was I willing to leave those far behind me and press on toward the mark?

Pride:

Pride is probably the underlying root sin of all of the above, and each of us is susceptible to it. The awful thing about pride is that others see it in us clearly while we are blinded to it personally.

The desire to have an image, and to try to be something that we are not is personally devastating. Pride deepens insecurity.

The antidote for pride is humility. I humbled myself before God and the staff in the Port Haven. I certainly didn't want to face a judge full of the blindness of pride.

Uncertainty in Primary Relationships:

Two of my working relationships were not secure. I didn't know where I stood. It seemed that I couldn't please regardless of what I did. I felt that I was a prisoner of certain expectations. Yet I didn't clearly know what those expectations were, so I was unable to fulfill them.

I felt trapped. I was unable to understand clearly what I was to do, so I was unable to face action.

It didn't matter whose fault it was. I loved those people dearly. I had proven that many times. Yet, when misunderstandings came, they always arrived at the most inconvenient times.

I was only responsible for my part, but I was 100 percent responsible for that. I would go again to the place of prayer and ask God to work in my life. Only He could place those most precious of relationships on a firm foundation once again.

Miscommunication:

Much insecurity results from wrong or misunderstood communication. Somehow I took comfort in this possible cause. Had I not learned from my childhood to be candid and speak what I thought? Yet I was to learn that there is much more to communication than what we say. How we say something is just as important as the words communicated. Then there is body language—the way we sit, look, stand, or gesture when we communicate.

The antidote for miscommunication is consistent, loving, open talking. Not verbosity, but concise, clear, wise words that say exactly what we mean. Proverbs states that a word fitly spoken is like apples of gold in settings of silver. That describes wise, timely communication. And it provides for secure relationships, whether among husband and wife, pastor and parishioner, employer and employee, father and child, brother and sister, or friend among friends.

Lack of Discipline and Encouragement:

Discipline is the shepherd's staff of relationships. Discipline keeps us from the precipice of disaster. It is like the fence around beautiful paddocks. Where discipline is lacking, the recipients are exposed to all sorts of poisonous plants.

Again, pastors and coaches, as well as executives, know that only a well-disciplined team produces desired results. Undisciplined members of any team can destroy years of work.

Encouragement is the safety net of relationships. Only when we are encouraged with proper incentives will we try, and keep on trying until we succeed.

Some executives will do more for a word of praise from the boss than for a doubled salary. Athletic coaches know the power of a word of encouragement. Pastors know all too well the need for positive reinforcement after a week in the troubled world.

Even conviction is encouraging to the biblical Christian as he realizes that God is dealing with his negative behavior. Correct behavior brings fulfillment to relationships with God and fellowman.

It seemed a long list.

I looked around the room at those sitting there. Each of us had personal weaknesses that were now being dealt with. How good of God to allow a time like this before we faced together the possibility of prison!

One of the group asked a profound question. When are we most likely to be insecure? More answers began to come.

Of course! It made sense to all of us. I was quite naturally facing a period of insecurity because the risks in this Greek trial were considerable. I had gone over a long inventory of consequences many times. Yet I knew that I did not go alone.

There were many possibilities, but the message God had for me was clear: *Trust Him.* That was exactly what I meant to do. I began to see the privilege of standing trial for the gospel. I also began to realize that perhaps we could bring freedom to that ancient birthplace of democracy. Freedom of conscience. Freedom of worship. Freedom from repressive laws.

The next morning I boarded the Pan Am flight to Geneva, then on to Athens. I picked up *These Fifteen*, the little gray paperback, from my briefcase. I had been deeply involved in the mental thinking of contingency plans and future implications. I was so looking forward to some light entertainment.

When I pulled the book up from the floor and opened the cover, I realized that this was not to be light or entertaining! It would be a message from history, used of God to further prepare me for His service in Athens.

I had long been an admirer of the Moravians. They brought the forgotten charge of missions to the foreground of the Protestant Church. They were also influential in the conversion and fire of the Wesleys.

The first chapter began on page 9. It was the story of John Hus, the Catholic who was a reformer before the Reformation. He was Professor of Philosophy at the University of Prague and eventually became a priest.

The passage that gripped me was his trial at Constance. Here was a man who remained firm in his convictions, even though death would be his reward. As his trial began there was an eclipse of the sun and the city of Constance had to be lighted for the trial to go on. Some would later say that this was an indication of impending doom for the Czechoslovakian hero. Others would explain that the darkness symbolized the state of heart of his accusers.

Eventually he was condemned. He was sentenced to death by burning at the stake. The description went deep into my heart.

> He was ordered to put on some priestly garments, which were promptly torn off. Next a communion cup or chalice was given to him, which only a priest might use, but it too was snatched away to show that he was no longer a priest. Then he was turned over to the State for proper punishment. A tall fool's cap, decorated with a picture of three devils fighting for his soul, was placed on his head. A thousand soldiers cleared the way and he was marched to the place of execution. As the procession passed the city square, he saw a huge bonfire in which copies of his books were being burned. They continued to the outside of the town, to an open field, where a stake had been driven firmly into the ground. To this Hus was bound with wet ropes. Straw and wood were piled around him, and once more he

was asked whether he would recant.
Never for a moment did his courage fail
him, and he declared, "I shall die with joy,
in the faith of the gospel which I have
preached" (Edwin A. Sawyer, *These Fifteen,* Comenius Press, 1963, p.14).

When the torch was applied and the smoke began
to rise, John Hus was heard reciting words from
the 31st and 51st Psalms. His last words were from
a Latin hymn that he began to sing: "Christ, Thou
Son of the living God, have mercy upon us." Then
the flames were blown into his face and he was
with Christ.

He gave his life for reform in the church. Today
he is honored, but then it cost him his life.

As I read through the passage in this little book,
I wept. I didn't care who was in the plane. This
man's life touched me. On the one hand, I wanted
to return home immediately. On the other hand,
courage welled up within me, not from my own
resources but from above. The truth of Matthew
10 was impressed upon my mind. When we are
brought before magistrates, judges, and rulers for
His name's sake, we need not fear what to say or
how to say it.

God would be with us.

I read on in the little book. Almost every one of
the 15 pioneers had been imprisoned. Several lost
their lives.

The more I read, the more I was challenged.

Seated on the plane, I opened my Bible for my
daily reading. I was still searching for a word of
comfort. But through consistent daily reading of His

Word, God feeds us what we need for sustenance. His menu choice is always superior to ours. And comfort was not what He had in mind for me.

I had taken a new Bible with me on the trip. I didn't want anything to happen to my well-marked, personal one. It has much of the last several years of my personal history marked in the margins as I have turned again and again to the Word for insight.

I opened the new Bible with the bookmark for my New Testament reading. It was Ephesians 3. My eye fell on the first few words of the chapter:

> For this reason I, Paul, the PRISONER OF CHRIST JESUS for the sake of you Gentiles... (NIV).

This was *not* what I wanted to read. I was looking for something about peace and safety or success and blessing.

Like many Christians, I kept on reading, hopeful that I would come across some passage that better suited my frame of mind. The truth of that first verse had penetrated deeply, yet I was still reaching. Where was a thread of direction that this trial in Greece would be dismissed as a domestic conflict between a husband and his former wife?

The following chapter began in almost the identical way.

> As a PRISONER FOR THE LORD, then, I urge you to live a life worthy of the calling you have received. Be completely humble and gentle; be patient, bearing

with one another in love. Make every effort to keep the unity of the Spirit through the bond of peace (NIV).

These passages are marked in ink in the margin of my Bible. The date is December 19, 1984. That was two days before the trial, on December 21 and 22. God was certainly speaking about prison.

This was consistent with how God has historically worked in people's lives. Paul had Agabus come and tie his hands with a cord, prophesying that Paul would be arrested in Jerusalem. Paul already knew that this was a possibility. God had prepared him. Agabus had no other source of information besides God. The prison sentence of Paul was confirmed through witnesses before he was even arrested.

For the last several months, I had been experiencing a rather perplexing thing in prayer. Often I ask the Lord to speak into my life when I am in need of direction. Time after time I felt impressed by the Holy Spirit to read Acts 12.

This chapter is primarily about Peter's imprisonment. I thought perhaps there was some message that God would give me from this historical account of Peter's jailing and the miraculous release. However, as I read and reread the passage, I didn't seem to be finding any message in this chapter at all. I was thinking of a teaching passage that I was to use in instructing others, but God wasn't wanting me to think of teaching others. He was preparing me. Preparing me for the possibility of prison!

I began to list the men who had been imprisoned in the will of God.

Joseph:

Prison was part of the preparation and development of God in Joseph's life. Man meant it for evil, but God used it for good. Joseph must have wondered about the dreams of his youth.

It would have been so easy to deny those dreams. He thought God had spoken through dreams that he would deliver his family. He thought God had said that he would be given a position above his brothers. And he told those older brothers that dream. No wonder he encountered their jealousy!

Yes, God did bring to pass all that He had told Joseph in a dream. But it required prison.

Jeremiah:

He was imprisoned because the authorities of his day didn't like his preaching. He was too straight. He spoke what needed to be said, regardless of the consequences, fearlessly. To the king. To the army. Anywhere.

And he ended up in prison.

I couldn't help but think of the parallels in modern society. We will only have true freedom if some people are prepared to lose their freedom for the sake of freedom.

Daniel:

He was a man of convictions, not of preference. Sometimes we are so compromising, always posturing for approval. Daniel was willing to suffer disapproval. He had convictions. His convictions were not just personal preferences. He would quietly go to his regular place of prayer even though the ruling government forbade it. He would not lead in public rebellion but quietly honored his God. That action cost him a prison sentence. It should have cost his life, but God intervened, and it became one of Daniel's greatest victories.

Samson:

The man was mighty, yet, he will forever be remembered for his failure with a woman. He is most often thought of as the strong man with a weakness, and that weakness cost him his leadership and put him in prison. But God remembered him, and in his death he was more victorious than in all his life. Prison was the crucible that made the difference.

Paul:

I thought of this mighty man who so shaped the theology of the church through his missionary letters. Many of those letters were written from prison. In Philippians 1:12-14 Paul writes:

> Now I want you to know, brothers, that what has happened to me has really served to advance the gospel. As a result, it has become clear throughout the whole palace guard and to everyone else that I am in chains for Christ. Because of my chains, most of the brothers in the Lord have been encouraged to speak the word

of God more courageously and fear-lessly (NIV).

Paul was very clear as to *why* he was in prison. God had placed him there; he was in chains for Christ.

At the close of the letter to the Philippians he sent greetings from the converts in jail. How would you like to be chained to the apostle Paul on a four-hour prison watch? Paul probably thanked God each time the prison watch was changed. A new shift of prison guards coming to work meant a new captive congregation to hear why he was in chains. He was in chains for Christ and no other reason.

I couldn't help but think of more recent world history.

Solzhenitsyn:

This twentieth-century prophet who pens the volumes that shake the foundations of power, both East and West, found his destiny in the prison experience.

A Jewish doctor explained to the cancer patient, Solzhenitsyn, the meaning of forgiveness and moral law. The acts of Christian charity which were lived out at such extreme cost, penetrated the brilliant young mind. God would use that inquisitive mind to write books reminiscent of Jeremiah's ancient messages.

The Waldensians:

These early God-fearing people were also a

minority church. I don't know how they would have survived in a country like Greece. There the dominant denomination controls 99 percent of the property and greatly influences the laws. These efforts maintain token control of the largely secular society.

The Waldensians were a major influence in the twelfth and thirteenth centuries. They can still be found today in the high alpine valleys of Northern Italy, especially along the French border.

It was the Waldensians, followers of a godly man named Waldo, who collected money so that the very first French Bible could be translated and published. The money was given to Farel and Salviotti, who were early reformers in French-speaking Switzerland.

In one long winter, under intense persecution (by those who allowed no tolerance for worship different from their own), 10,000 of these believers perished on the slopes of the French Alps. They were fleeing for their lives.

The Swiss who lived across the Lake of Geneva hoisted the sails on their small fishing craft by night, braving the perilous winds that could swamp their small craft, and plied the waters to the French coastal towns. They loaded the boats as fully as they dared and sailed to the Swiss town of Nyon. There the Waldensians found safety and tolerance.

And it was out of gratitude to the Swiss for saving some of their fellow believers that they graciously provided the funds to translate the Bible from Latin into the commonly spoken French.

The parallel here with our situation in Athens begs to be explained.

The Bible that was given to young Konstantine Koutopolon that fateful day after the earthquake was the world-famous Living Bible. It had been recently paraphrased into the modern Greek language.

The current Old Testament version of the Greek Bible is the Septuagint, a translation from Hebrew to Greek done in the second century before Christ. It is probably the oldest language translation in use today. Unfortunately, even the most basic of words have changed, and the Septuagint is not at all understandable to the vast majority of Greek youth. Part of this is a language problem. Another part reflects the natural movement of an ancient Mediterranean society, the Greek society, into the twentieth-century world. These changes are neither easy nor painless. One aspect of the battle that is being waged in Greece today has to do with the Living Bible and its popular usage.

The Puritans:

I have already referred to the Puritans, who so greatly shaped the early history of the United States of America. They were also commonly called "Separatists."

In the 1600's they were persecuted in England because, like so many others, they held a minority view.

Our early American forefathers had to leave England because of the intolerance of government and religious officials. Their lifestyle, faith, and commitment were too stark a contrast for the seared consciences of some of the opposition. In

1618 the King of England issued an edict commanding all Separatists (Puritans) not conforming to ecclesiastical authority to leave England.

This simply meant that in order for the Puritans to build a church to worship in, they had to have written authorization from the Bishop of the Church of England. This occurred almost a hundred years before the revivals of Wesley and Whitefield. The legal actions of Wilberforce had not yet revolutionized England and the Church.

No self-respecting Puritan would even think of asking the Bishop of a corrupt state church for permission to worship or build a house of worship. Intolerance was rampant on both sides. The only alternative was the Mayflower and the New World.

Had our God-fearing forefathers not persisted even in the face of trials, our destiny would have been affected. But in and through these trials, they gave birth to a 200-year-old tradition: Thanksgiving Day. Thanks be to God for His faithfulness and divine providence!

Twenty years ago, American students studied this in their history books. Now the influence of Fabian Socialism and the resulting humanism has eradicated all references to God. Sadly, early American history is being rewritten.

Now my Pan Am flight circled the Swiss and French Alps. Below was the historic city of Geneva. Snow covered the alpine slopes where the Waldensians had fled some 300 years earlier. I could easily see how so many lost their lives.

Lausanne was visible in the distance. More than 700 years old, Lausanne's cathedral is perched above the city and looks over the apartment houses that terrace the many hills. This cathedral and the small stone building beside it saw more than 400 of its young men and women sent to France, where they would be martyred for their faith. That small stone building was the training center of the French Protestant movement. These two cities were the very center of the Reformed tradition.

Memories again flooded my mind as the plane approached the runway at Cointrin, the Aeroport de Geneve, on the border between France and the city of the 22nd Canton of Switzerland. My two oldest children were born here. Many friends were here. What would they think of my going to trial and possibly prison in Greece?

I would spend only the one night in Lausanne, breaking the long journey from Honolulu en route to Athens. I wanted to see at least a few of my Swiss friends. It would be good to see Pierre, Bruno, Heinz, Rudi, and the others.

Pierre was certain that I was doing the wrong thing. He didn't want me to go back to Greece. I understood his concern and realized that it was his way of expressing his love for me.

It had been my privilege to lead Pierre to the Lord. I marveled at the growth in him. He had been visiting the prisons in the area, passing out Bibles with the Gideon Society as well as attending and leading Bible studies. This was certainly not the Pierre of a few years earlier!

Pierre could hardly wait to relate to me how just the previous weekend he had gone to the prison of Geneva and witnessed to several men in the cells. I could sense his tenderness as he related how their lives opened up to him as he told them about the One who had suffered the greatest injustice of all. Pierre knelt beside one inmate and led him through a prayer of repentance. He was now a new brother in Christ.

God is so faithful! For me to see a multiplication of people in the kingdom of God through one that I have personally led to Christ is a special joy. Praise God! I was so grateful that Pierre had remained on his knees and not quit.

I left Pierre's home in Chigny and drove on up to the place that had been our home for so long. The mission center at Chalet-a-Gobet looked much like a large Swiss chalet. It stood there nestled against the forest. Many times I had taken prayer walks in the forest, getting to know the Lord. It was here that Deyon and I were students upon arriving in Europe after our theological training.

Rudi and Eliane, our first Swiss in the mission, were leading the work, and they asked me to speak to the staff and students. I also stopped by the mercy ships' European office and spoke there. They were all standing with me in prayer.

Finally I boarded an Olympic Airways flight. The plane was packed with Athens-bound Greeks. I was in the center of the aircraft, with everyone speaking Greek around me.

I so love the Greek people. Their open, warm personalities melt any reserve in my heart. It is said that once you have a Greek friend, you have a friend for life, and once you have a Greek enemy, you have an enemy for life.

The plane landed in Athens at the Helenikon Airport. After customs I began to look for the most dynamic Greek I have ever met. I went outside for a bit, then back inside. And there he was. Costas Macris! With him was his wife, Alcay, and several of their children. I did so love this man! He was a true missionary hero. And his family was such a joy to be with.

Costas and his family had been missionaries in Indonesia among the Dani tribe of Irian Jaya. He had done an outstanding work among a primitive people. He had come back to his native Greece after 16 years in primitive conditions, and only then because of a severe case of hepatitis and related conditions.

When I first met him he still looked jaundiced. His spirit and feet were in action, but his body had trouble keeping up with his mind and heart.

He loved his native Athens and the Greece of his forebears. He was a member of the First Evangelical Church of Athens. This church was affiliated with the Presbyterian and Reformed Churches and was Athens' oldest Protestant church. Even though John Calvin would not appreciate any church following his pure doctrine being called heretical, these evangelicals are considered just that!

I would be a houseguest of the Macris family during the days before the trial and during the trial itself.

Alan Williams was already in Athens and had counseled with the attorney recommended by the British Embassy. Alan had met with him several weeks before and had found that he was also well spoken of by the American Embassy.

Most people we talked to seemed to think this was simply a domestic issue brought by a woman who had divorced her husband. She was using the three of us as tools for her vindictiveness.

As we met together in Costas' office at the Hellenic Missionary Union, I was troubled. We were prepared legally. Costas especially, being Greek, had done his homework. But were we really prepared spiritually?

Oh, certainly we had all prayed. But what should we do if we were condemned?

The three of us discussed the matter. I had a strong sense that we should insist on prison if found guilty. Alan and Costas agreed. Greek law allowed a prison sentence of up to four months to be voided by payment of a fine. We believed that if found guilty, it would be more honoring to the Lord to serve the imprisonment than pay the fine.

The world needed to know that Christians were being prevented from following Christ in the very center of Christendom. But at this stage, the worst scenario we could imagine was four months in prison. Little did we realize that we would be sentenced to prison for 3½ years!

CHAPTER
TWELVE

I woke early, after only a few hour's sleep, in Costas' Athens apartment. His son Jonathan had flown from Moody Bible Institute to be with his father. Their family was so close and wholesome!

In true Mediterranean fashion, the family often ate the main meal between eight and ten in the evening, remaining in conversation until midnight or even later. I was on jet lag and awoke shortly after they had gone to bed.

Today was December 21, 1984, the day of the trial.

I read the passages from the book of Acts that described the apostle Paul on trial. These powerful scriptural accounts gave me a pattern for my defense.

Paul prayed for courage while he awaited his trial in Rome. I could now better understand his need for inner strength. I too prayed for boldness and courage. I thought of my heavenly Father. He would be watching closely throughout the entire trial. I wanted Him to be pleased with His sons. I prayed for the others, Alan and Costas. I prayed for unity among the local believers. I prayed for their strength, too.

It was cold and wintry in Athens. I was glad that Deyon had packed the warm clothing. The wool cardigan and wool jacket would still require a winter overcoat for the more shadowy hours of the day.

I breakfasted with the entire Macris family.

No one really knew what to expect. We were all fully aware of the trial's importance to all the evangelicals in the country. Perhaps, just perhaps, God would allow this case to change the laws and history of Greece!

We were required to be in the courtroom by nine that morning. Jonathan drove us by Costas' office first to get all the paperwork, and then we went to downtown Athens.

We were informed that we would have to wait until our case was called. We were number 30. If our case was not called, we would have to wait several weeks in Athens until it was rescheduled. I found myself in the amusing position of actually praying that I be brought to trial that day!

There were rumors of a strike by the clerks in the court. Perhaps the case would be postponed. I prayed again. I called to Alan, and together we prayed that the trial would take place that very day.

Finally Alan and I simply went into a cafe and ordered the local Turkish coffee. We would eventually wait until three in the afternoon for our trial to begin.

I looked up at the Parthenon above the city. Again I remembered the high esteem once historically held for the open exchange of ideas and debate. Paul had given his famous Mars Hill message just a short distance from the Parthenon.

The day was not bright and cheery like our past Aegean summers. The sky was gray and dismal. It was the perfect day for a sense of foreboding, and a deep desire to be elsewhere. Thank You, Lord, that I'm not facing this alone! I was grateful for the two high-caliber, dedicated men standing with me.

Soon after we returned to the judicial building, our number was up. It was time. We made our way into the courtroom.

The trial began.

Our case was number 30 of the 35 to be heard that day. The remaining five were postponed and scheduled for another time. Our case would be held over for an unprecedented, special Saturday session that would last until ten in the evening.

Konstantine's mother, the woman who had brought us to trial, was first called to the witness stand. She spent the next few hours explaining how corrupt and terrible the three of us were.

The mercy ship kidnapped children. Unimaginable orgies occurred on board. We were financed by the CIA. We were all involved in some international plot to steal her son. We had ruined him. He now read his Bible. He didn't participate in premarital sex. The only time he was out late was attending Bible studies and meetings with other like-minded fanatics.

The defense attorney moved for a mistrial. A

miscarriage of justice was about to happen.

Konstantine Koutopolon was now 19. He was an adult under Greek law. He lived at home with his father, who had remarried. He worked in his father's business. He had never left Greece.

The ship had sailed more than 3½ years ago. We had never been summoned to the trial or informed of the charges against us. Was this some sort of vendetta or crusade that the mother had launched? What influence and finance had encouraged her to do this? She had been featured on the front page of the leftist daily paper. Was this part of the swing to the left of the population of Greece? What was the real reason behind the trial?

One of the charges was "Attempted kidnapping."

How could anyone be accused of attempted kidnapping when the person was still in Greece, with his father?

Mrs. Douka railed on. She testified that if her son would disavow all belief in God, the church, and the Bible, and became a radical Communist, that would be permissible. But he could *not* become a committed Christian.

The defense attorney moved again for a mistrial. Konstantine was an adult. He alone could bring charges against us. He obviously denied his mother's testimony.

The judge overruled the motion. The trial would go on.

The second charge was "proselytism."

Proselytism!

This was the centuries-old Greek words for conversion. To evangelize or spread the good news, resulting in a change of heart, was to proselytize. Every biblical Christian should be guilty of this, or his faith was of little effect!

How could the Greek government forbid the very techniques that the apostle Paul had used in founding the first Christian churches in Athens and Corinth?

Konstantine had not been baptized in any other church. He was born in the ancient land of the first European Christians. He was not Moslem, Hindu, or Buddhist. He was simply a twentieth-century humanistic youth who did not know the God of his forebears. He had come to living faith. Christ had changed his heart.

And that was a crime?

All of a sudden it was clear: We were fighting a far greater battle. It truly *was* spiritual warfare. If it is illegal to speak about Christ in such a way that a person is converted to believing, biblical Christianity, then we were being forbidden to do exactly what Christ had commanded.

> This gospel of the kingdom will be preached in the whole world as a testimony to all nations, and then the end will come'' (Matthew 24:14 NIV).

We must proclaim. People will believe. Hearts will be changed. Proselytism will occur. Whole nations will be converted.

The Greeks themselves were among the most active proselytizers in the third, fourth, and following centuries. Early evangelists had gone to Balkan peoples and far into the Caucases mountains with this same message that we had proclaimed in the village squares.

Like them, we too were commanded by Jesus to go spread the news.

The United Nations charter guarantees the right of religious assembly and the open exchange of religious convictions. How could Greece, the mother of democracy, take such drastic measures to restrict the very preaching made so famous on Mars Hill?

Of course preaching, proclaiming, teaching, doing good, and helping with two hands results in conversion. It stands as a Gibraltar of contrast against the evil manipulation of modern society.

The earliest Christian groups spread out around the world. Converts were the expected results. England left her Druids behind. Scandinavia quit marauding as Vikings and drinking the blood of slain victims from the skulls of previous conquests. The cannibalistic acts of the South Pacific were forgotten as they followed kings and chiefs in conversion to follow Jesus.

But during the trial we heard of Greek pastors who were fined, threatened with imprisonment, and jailed for preaching the gospel of peace. Alan and I were the first non-Greeks to face such charges in recent history.

Our sentence was 3½ years. This constitutes the longest sentence for anything of this nature since the overthrow of the Turkish Ottoman Empire, in 1823. It is the longest sentence for preaching since modern Greece became an independent country.

No one was more surprised than I when the presiding judge sentenced us and then set us free pending an appeal. I had expected to go to jail. At least I thought we would have to surrender our passports and be required to remain in Athens. Yet the judge let us go.

Was God allowing us to stand with the many other minority groups in Greece that had been victimized for decades by the same laws? Was this an opportunity to see the laws changed?

Research revealed that these laws were written under the former Metaxes dictatorship of 1938-39. Most of the repressive regulations of this era have been rewritten in the last ten years. But this particular law was left on the books.

And by its continuing authority, we were being forbidden to follow Jesus.

Our only reason for being in the country had been to repair a ship. Our only real crime was assisting those who were suffering after an earthquake. Our only criminal act was to give a Bible to a lonely boy. His only crime was that his heart was changed. He began to know the God of history.

If we had to do it all over again, what would we do differently?

We would do our best to give out more Bibles and pray with more troubled, lonely people. We would try harder. We would work with greater intensity and act with fuller obedience.

We would follow Jesus.

I remembered a poem sent to me by a lady in Zimbabwe just before I came to Greece for the trial.

> I know we'll stand before the judgment
> seat someday;

I often wondered what our Lord would
have to say.

"Well done, My child—you accepted Me;
You are guiltless—you may now go free."
And yet I think there's so much more to
be accounted for:
Suppose we stand before His throne this
very day
And hear what the Lord has to say.

"My child, I dwelt in you, in all My
power and glory too.
I commissioned you to preach My Word.
I ask you now—how many people heard?
You were My hands to heal the sick,
My voice to calm their fears . . . I ask you
now,
Were those productive years?
So many times My heart ached with pain
To see the lost so damned—
so many, many people from every race
and land.
Enter your rest now, My child,
But be not beguiled.
There was so much more for you to do,
When others could have seen Me in you.
It's too late now.
Completed!
Done!
Those that are lost are lost—and—
Those that are won are won!"

—Author Unknown by man
but known by God

I don't want to stand before the Lord and hear Him say that there was much more I could have done.

A local Athens pastor invited me to speak on the Sunday morning after the trial. I accepted, knowing that I could go by the church and then on to the airport. Hopefully I would find a seat and be home for Christmas Day.

Alan and I stood together there in one of Athens' fastest-growing churches. Here was real spiritual life. Many in the congregation were new converts won in the last few years. Here was a sure sign of hunger for God. Several of the new believers were friends from the ministry of the Anastasis. I wondered how many times we could be brought to trial for proselytism! Praise be to God! Here was a lot more evidence.

That small, flickering flame sparked at the opening of the trial was about to burst into full, furnace intensity among these people. This small minority of committed biblical Christians were just like the minority that changed the corrupt Roman society 1500 years ago.

They were like the Moravians, the early Reformers, the Waldensians, the Puritans. Somewhere among them was a young Wilberforce, who would be used to change the laws of the land, freeing the slaves of conscience. Would there be a young John Wesley or Whitefield, who, through the preaching of the Word, would bring about the greatest sociological change of society?

This was the reason we had come back for the trial. This was why we would also return for the appeal.

The love of the brethren—that was reason enough. We could not abandon them. The case for Christianity was now internationalized. Perhaps the Greek laws could be changed through international efforts and public support. Then Presbyterians, Catholics, Baptists, Pentecostals, Brethren, and Lutheran believers would no longer be considered heretics.

The church in Athens was praying for our case. Several of them had been standing in the courtroom during the 15-hour trial, and I was fully aware of their support.

Somehow our being there gave them courage. And their prayerful support gave us new strength.

I said goodbye and made my way to the Helenikon airport. A Lufthansa plane was leaving for Frankfurt. There I might possibly find a Pan Am flight to wing me to my family in Hawaii.

On the same plane was Helmut Grundman, the President of the European Evangelical Alliance. He had attended the entire trial, representing the evangelicals of all of Europe. These same churches in the rest of Europe were the major representation of Christendom. Only in Greece were they heretics.

Mr. Grundman was acquainted with the work of YWAM, as he was secretary for another mission in Germany. We had several mutual friends. As we turned our talk to the trial, Mr. Grundman compared the lack of religious liberty in Greece to the repression of the Soviet Bloc. "Only there can similar persecution of religious minorities be found," he said, shaking his head. We parted in Frankfurt.

There I telephoned Deyon.

She had gathered the children around for a devotional time. They were busy preparing for Christmas, painfully aware of the absence of their father. Deyon was making every effort to point to what Jesus had done for us. She was stressing that if we are called upon to suffer for Him, He will give us grace—not just to Dad, but to everyone in the family. She related that Heidi and Luke seemed to have the greatest comprehension of the situation because of their age.

And with or without Dad, it was time to give gifts.

In our family we often give a gift to the Lord on Christmas. We have done this for years. Something memorized. Something made for Him, like a Scripture to be placed for decoration. Perhaps a commitment of time to do something for others in His name. These were the kinds of presents we normally gave Him at His birthday.

This year Deyon asked the two eldest children to do something special. They didn't know if their father would be in prison or free. Then, when they heard I was free, it still looked as though I would miss Christmas.

Deyon asked each of them to offer their father's absence as a gift to the Lord.

Heidi first, then Luke, prayed a prayer of relinquishment, remembering how Jesus had left His home to come for all of mankind. The reluctant and emotional words came from both their mouths. They gave me back to the Lord.

And He, in turn, gave me back to them. The airlines had a seat open the next day. If I flew through the night and all day, making the connecting flights, I would make it just in time to be home for Christmas. Our joy was understandable when we were reunited on Christmas day!

I began to strategize for the future with the various options open to me. I was in a situation I had never before encountered. The stark realization of having to prepare myself for possible imprisonment was often in my prayers and thoughts.

The Greek courts would send us the legal writ explaining their condemnation, and the case would be tried again in a higher court. The date was not set and would depend upon the court schedule and the national elections.

Of course I would go back. I must. Alan agreed. We would stand with Costas and all the others in Greece.

I would have to prepare the mercy ships for a possible lengthy absence. Both ships would need interim, additional leadership. God had already been preparing two men for these roles.

I would have to prepare my family. I would devote quality time to each child. And every moment with Deyon would become a very precious commodity.

Finally, I would have to prepare myself. "Guilty!" the judge had said. "I sentence you to 3½ years in prison!"

How does a person prepare himself for prison?